WYNTER AND
JONATHAN PITTS

HARVEST HOUSE PUBLISHERS
EUGENE, OREGON

Cover by Emily Weigel Design

Cover photo © Dariusz Gudowicz / Shutterstock

Emptied

Copyright © 2019 Wynter Pitts and Jonathan Pitts
Published by Harvest House Publishers
Eugene, Oregon 97408
www.harvesthousepublishers.com

ISBN 978-0-7369-7041-9 (pbk.)
ISBN 978-0-7369-7042-6 (eBook)

Library of Congress Cataloging-in-Publication Data
Names: Pitts, Wynter, author.
Title: Emptied / Wynter and Jonathan Pitts.
Description: Eugene : Harvest House Publishers, 2018.
Identifiers: LCCN 2018030164 (print) | LCCN 2018035747 (ebook) | ISBN 9780736970426 (ebook) | ISBN 9780736970419 (pbk.)
Subjects: LCSH: Marriage--Religious aspects--Christianity.
Classification: LCC BV835 (ebook) | LCC BV835 .P58 2018 (print) | DDC 248.8/44--dc23
LC record available at https://lccn.loc.gov/2018030164

Printed in the United States of America
18 19 20 21 22 23 24 25 26 / BP-GL / 10 9 8 7 6 5 4 3 2 1

Contents

This book is dedicated to the ones that showed us the way. To Viola Carter, whose strength, faith, and endurance were met with God's goodness. And to Garry and Miriam Pitts for their selfless and intentional love, fought for with sacrifice and deference. We are grateful that you poured out your lives in plain sight. You are imperfect, yet perfect, examples of the Lord Jesus Himself in our eyes.

Foreword

A few months back, Rebekah and I were wrapping up lunch together in a crowded restaurant. As we were signing the check and adding gratuity, we overheard a man at a nearby table make the kind of hyperbolic statement that would stop any married couple in their tracks.

"My wife and I just celebrated 42 years of marriage, and *we've never once raised our voice with one another.*"

Seriously?

He went on to add, "Of course, we've had a few disagreements over the years. But we always work through them rather easily." Our mouths dropped open. We didn't know that was a thing.

This random couple—strangers to us—unknowingly were recasting our imagination for a healthy marriage only half as far along. Our 21-year journey together is an incredible testimony to what God can do through selflessness and commitment, even when our voices have hit full crescendos.

If we had been thinking through it, we would have cancelled our planned meetings, pulled up our chairs, and asked them dozens of questions; prodding them all afternoon for every little bit of advice, nugget of truth, and lasting encouragement that could help us say the same of our next 21 years. What a missed opportunity.

Even though that moment slipped by for us, your moment doesn't have to.

In the pages ahead, Wynter and Jonathan invite us to a seat at their table. By revealing personal stories and courageously exposing their early failings and misguided expectations, they graciously welcome us into their story—a journey of learning, healing, and loving one another God's way. Their bold, honest, and transparent thoughts will encourage your heart. What we would have given for mentors like this during our earliest years of marriage!

Whether you find yourself in a good marriage or a strained marriage or are contemplating marriage, this book is meant for you. Through Jonathan and Wynter's fun, winsome, and vulnerable words, you will learn that marriage is an all-out commitment—demanding the sincere effort of both partners with an invitation for God's supernatural intervention during all seasons.

What we are most thankful for is their courage to let us in on the good, the bad, and the ugly. With a united voice they encourage us all to keep moving forward, renew our marriages in the truths of Scripture, and never let it be an option to walk away.

Now pull up your chair and engage in a conversation that will have lasting significance.

Gabe and Rebekah Lyons
Authors and Founders of Q

Before you Begin

A Special Note from Jonathan

At 3:45 p.m. on July 24, 2018, I hit *send* on an e-mail to our publisher with the final, edited manuscript of this book attached. Around 7:30 p.m. on that same July day, Wynter breathed her last breath as I desperately tried to save it.

It never crossed my mind how God would use the sending of that e-mail to encourage my heart on the most difficult day I have ever faced—and in the weeks and months to follow.

It was a proud moment and a relief for sure. Wynter and I had been laboring through the writing process for several months, doing our best to capture our story in a way that would speak to engaged couples, young marrieds, and anyone looking for a new outlook on marriage. We had a sense of accomplishment and truly believed that God was going to work through our story to reach others who might identify with our journey.

It was a neat experience for us to write the book because in a lot of ways we felt we were stepping into a new season of marriage. As husband and wife, we had grown together. We were both committed to a type of marriage that would focus on the other person. Though we came to our marriage with different backgrounds and expectations, we daily practiced the discipline of a godly marriage. We practiced because we never felt like professionals. What we lacked in profession, we made up with intention. Along the way, we realized we were picking up younger couples whom God would allow us to pour our lives into. Our intentions were shifting theirs.

Intention. I'm grateful I can say without pause that we were intentional. Without question we were deliberate about pursuing fullness in marriage. Each day Wynter and I would find opportunities to pour ourselves out for each other, and each day God would fill us with more and more of His power to do it again the next. And in His power, we experienced the fullness in marriage only God can give.

Even while Wynter's heart was full of gratitude and excitement about our new journey, in a moment her physical heart failed her without warning. On that day she started a new journey with a new eternal reality, trusting God with me and our four girls left here on earth.

Her sudden death was gut-wrenching and heartbreaking. It was beyond reason and beyond understanding. She was 38. We had celebrated our fifteenth anniversary less than a month earlier on June 27.

But God, in his infinite wisdom, sent me signs of His goodness despite my lack of human understanding. In His providence and foresight, He allowed me to turn in our marriage book the same day Wynter passed from death to life. He was reminding me and anyone looking on that He is the author, and that as the author He decides when the book will end.

Wynter's life is an amazing book. Much of it you will learn from reading this one. God gifted her and used her to reach a generation of girls, moms, and families for His kingdom purposes. Likewise, our marriage was a good book. It was full of ups and downs, highs and lows, and the eventual resolve and excitement that comes in any great story. Just like a great story, our book seemed to end way too soon. And just like a reader, I sit here wishing I could experience more.

Despite the shortness of our book, I'm thankful I can say our story ended with a beautiful climax—including four beautiful memorials to Wynter in our daughters. I have no regrets, and I assure you that if Wynter could write, neither would she. We lived each day asking the Lord to "teach us to number our days, that we may gain a heart of wisdom." We had no idea how soon our journey would come to an end, but we lived each one as if it was numbered, pursuing the best for each other and offering our marriage up to God.

My hope is that Wynter's death will continue to bring life. That her story and our marriage will stand as a light on the path of your marriage—and that whatever might be dead or lost or unattended will begin to receive nourishment and sustenance. I pray that you might begin or commit anew to a poured-out marriage so that you might also experience the fullness promised from God for those who live out Christ to each other.

I'm not sure how long your book is, and I'm certain you aren't either. But I encourage you to make it a good one. To remember each day that the next is not promised, and that the one you have right now is the best one to lay down for each other in order to experience the fullness of a poured-out marriage.

The Key

Marital bliss. We all want it, and no one goes into marriage expecting less. Most boys expect it to just happen when they grow up, as if their sheer presence is the key ingredient to the marriage recipe. Many girls idealize marriage, symbolized by their growing fantasies about its inaugural day. Normally we memorialize this assumed bliss with a special wedding ceremony photo, but rarely does the image capture what the true state of our marriage relationship will be on a day-to-day basis.

For most of us, that masterpiece is nicely framed and gently placed somewhere like on the fireplace mantel, a perfect rendition of what we hoped for our marriage relationship. But in reality our marriages are more like the snapshots Great-Aunt Clara took during the wedding—a little blurry, with someone's head in the way and the bride in mid-sneeze. Day in and day out, we spend our energy desperately seeking that perfection, only to discover it's tucked away among a zillion other images far less perfect and flattering.

Not too long after framing that masterpiece, couples discover marriage is much more like a journey than a snapshot. It cannot be captured in a frame. It's a marathon, not a sprint. It will take more than they ever thought they could give, and it will test every aspect of their will.

We understand. We can relate. We are one of those couples.

Now, before you think we're going to rip our marriage or yours, please know that's not the route we're taking. We just happen to be a couple of realists who are passionate about pursuing the dream we both had in mind 15 years ago when that beautiful, black-and-white 8x10 photo that now sits on the fireplace mantel in our family room was taken. Thankfully, God has been gracious all along the way, opening our eyes and ultimately our hearts to begin painting a portrait much grander than we ever envisioned.

We are on the journey, committed to the pursuit of the dream God birthed in us when He pushed our paths together. But we've realized a few things along the way, and we want to share them with you.

Emptied. The word is simple, and we all understand it. In marriage, emptying ourselves is the key to unlocking what God had in mind to ultimately bring about what He has for you and for us in this most vital relationship.

We are to be emptied. More than that, we are to empty ourselves. But empty ourselves of what? Obviously, we can empty ourselves of only what fills us up. Which begs the question, *What are we full of?*

Real joy, real peace, and real happiness are found when we empty ourselves of *me*. We'll talk about that, but not simply for the sake of discussion. We have a purpose in mind—emptying ourselves of *me* as we work on becoming *we*. So often we come into our marriages with our own agendas, with our own desires. It's about what *I want* and what *I can get*. We make it about our own needs and expectations. But marriage at its best and in the right form rarely has its focus on self. It is other focused. It seems counterintuitive, but real joy, real peace, and real happiness are found when we empty ourselves of *me*.

In the pages ahead, we'll share our honest story of being emptied. You'll learn that some of our emptying was intentional, and some was forced. We'll share about how we brought a portrait into our marriage that was well intentioned and even God ordained, though living it out was not as automatic as we had hoped. We've learned and continue to learn that emptying ourselves is a daily decision. It's a journey. It's a way of life.

In the end, your emptiness is primarily where God can fill your marriage with the purpose, passion, and fullness He had in mind from the very beginning—and has in mind as He paints His masterpiece, one stroke at a time.

Part One

Poured Out

1

Hot and Ready

Wynter

H ot and ready. That's how I've always liked them.

I also prefer them perfectly round, slightly fluffy, and glazed with goodness. I'm talking about my donuts, of course.

I've never quite understood those who prefer donuts to be dense, almost cake-like, and I pray earnestly for the handful of souls who don't enjoy them at all! I believe desserts are my love language, and a nice hot donut is essential to my existence. Okay, so I may be exaggerating slightly, but when my now-husband invited me on an hour-long drive for a hot, sweet, and fluffy donut, I knew he was *the one.*

I guess you could say he had me at "donuts"! By the end of that first long drive, however, we offered each other a different taste of reality.

Here's the full story.

Jonathan and I met on our Philadelphia college campus in 2001, days away from entering our fourth year. Unlike most universities, the school we attended operated on a five-year program. We were both considered juniors with one year left to go.

I had just returned from studying abroad. I'd spent the last four months strolling streets in England, Italy, France, and Ireland, and I was convinced that returning to the States was temporary. My mind and heart were set on finishing my undergraduate degree and then returning to London to live. Notice I did not say to work or to study. Neither of those two things were the goal. I just wanted to live freely, touring the cities and working here and there as necessary in small coffee shops along cobblestone roads.

When I met Jonathan, unlike some of my peers, I wasn't interested in "finding a man." I liked to have fun, and I wasn't opposed to a free dinner, but I was self-focused. I'd grown self-sufficient, with little thought put into what a future would look like with anyone permanently by my side.

It wasn't always that way. When I was younger, I knew I wanted a family. Like most little girls, when I closed my eyes and pictured my future, the overwhelming vision in my head featured a husband, two kids (a boy and a girl, of course), and a dog. I dreamed of having what I didn't have then—a complete family.

I grew up in a single-parent home and a primarily female-dominated environment. As I grew older, I didn't ponder the term *husband* often, if at all. The idea of giving a male companion a consistent space in my life just didn't cross my mind. And considering the available options on my college campus, it became easy to push any idea of marriage, at least at that point in life, farther and farther into the distance. I figured any pieces I needed for my dream of happily-ever-after to become reality would come *after*. After what,

I wasn't sure, but it certainly wasn't on my agenda the evening I met Jonathan.

**I was immediately intrigued by Jonathan.
Something about this man drew me.**

There is no denying, however, that I was immediately intrigued by Jonathan. Something about this man drew me. It may have been his caramel-colored skin and that beautiful face of his! He was cute—really cute. But there was more.

We met at a house party, of all places, and I distinctly remember sitting in a room full of noisy people and noticing only him. He was funny. He was loud, too, yet despite his efforts to fit in with the other guys from his group, his kindness and good-hearted nature stood out. Thinking back on this night reminds me of the saying "You can take the boy out of the church, but you can't take the church out of the boy." I'm being a bit facetious, but I think this explains what my heart was drawn to that evening.

I should stop here to tell you that when Jonathan and I met, neither of us were following the biblical standards set for us in our childhood homes. Sure, Jonathan was in the gospel choir, and I occasionally ventured to a local church or an on-campus service, but neither of us were actively seeking to grow in our personal relationship with Jesus.

Yet I believe it was the very presence of God's love that attracted my heart to his almost immediately. When I think of the night Jonathan and I met, I can't help but thank God for His sovereignty. His hand was working out the details of my life and weaving the pieces together to accomplish His perfect will, despite my personal efforts or shortcomings. Jonathan was God's perfect gift for me, and I didn't even know it.

Jonathan

For me, it was love at first sight. I laid eyes on Wynter months before she ever noticed me. I have distinct and vivid memories of seeing her on numerous occasions during our third year, the year before we officially met. I would often be leaving my dorm for my first class of the day as she was heading back to her apartment from a class. I'm 100 percent sure she was oblivious to my presence then, because, as she mentioned, the first time she remembers seeing me is at a party a year later. I guess my face wasn't as memorable as hers.

> **Wynter's walk was a mix of poise and purpose. I didn't know where she was going, but I sure did want to follow.**

Wynter's walk was a mix of poise and purpose. I didn't know where she was going, but I sure did want to follow. Something about her captivated me, although I had zero confidence to ever approach her. In all honesty, and I joke about this on a routine basis, I didn't think I had much of a chance with her because she seemed to walk with a bit of a chip on her shoulder. To say it plainly, she looked a bit snooty.

Now, before you go judging me for my prejudgment of my wife, allow me to explain. Wynter is about as introverted as introversion gets. She has always been the most reserved person in the room. Though she's confident, she's quiet. And though she's purposeful, she's not boastful. All that contributed to her walking by my dorm looking as though she had little concern for what was going on around her. So I let it go. I chalked up my interest in her as a loss without ever building up the gumption to stop her and introduce myself.

Then on that momentous night at a party given by one of my closest friends, we finally met. Ironically, Wynter wasn't so quiet as we talked and danced. We ended the evening by exchanging phone numbers, and I had every intention of calling.

Continuing with the lack-of-confidence theme, however, I never did. It's not that I didn't want to, or that I wasn't interested. I guess you could say I was nervous, and over time it became easier and easier to push the risk of failure to the background.

But God had a plan, and it was realized through the stalkerlike tendencies of a quiet yet confident girl. Yep, you heard it right. Wynter was a stalker! Thankfully, that habit didn't last long, but God gave her just enough stalking ability to learn that we each had a class in the same building at the same time. She came early to class, which I soon realized wasn't typical for her, just so we would cross paths. She intentionally ran smack-dab into me, saying, "Hello," and waiting for my response. For days, I would say, "Hey, how are you?" and walk by, showing little interest in her. I crack up as I think about it now, and we've laughed together about it, but my confidence level was still zero.

Thankfully, Wynter's wasn't. One day she caught me off guard. She gave me her normal "Hello," and I played it cool with a casual reply. But instead of letting me walk away, this time she somewhat abrasively and confidently asked, "Why haven't you called me yet?"

Dumbfounded, I simply replied, "I don't know. I'll call you soon."

Wynter

Jonathan's rendition of our first introductions still makes me chuckle. Although his words are true, I feel the need to add a few details from my vantage point, starting with the fact that I wasn't a stalker.

Okay, maybe I was.

Please keep in mind, however, that we met long before the days of social media, so I had to track him down the old-fashioned way. I asked a friend for his schedule and strategically placed myself in his path—daily!

I did this because I knew Jonathan was, at the very least, intrigued by me as well. A few days after we exchanged phone numbers, a friend asked me about him. I told her he hadn't called yet, and she was just as baffled as I was. She said, "That's so weird, because I know he really liked you." A mutual friend of mine and Jonathan's had told her that, so I knew it had to be true.

Her words gave me the confidence I needed to get to the bottom of what was going on with him. Although we had spent only a few hours together, I knew almost immediately that something special was happening between us, and I couldn't understand why he wasn't responding. With this knowledge in my arsenal, I developed a plan for forward progress.

He finally seized the opportunity and called. We chatted for a bit about our families, our class schedules, and common campus life before the conversation lent itself to an invitation for the first of what would become our forever dates.

We went to see the movie *Monsters, Inc.* Nothing else we wanted to see was playing, but seeing it allowed us time to work through our nerves. Jonathan was so nervous that, when he dropped me off at my apartment afterward, he drove off before I could even get my keys out of my purse to unlock my door. In West Philadelphia. In the dark. Late at night. Not good.

It must not have taken Jonathan long to realize dessert was my sweet spot, because when he found out about a grand opening for a store in my favorite donut shop chain an hour away, he invited me to go there with him.

Back to hot and ready.

So thoughtful, right? He was a keeper, and I knew it.

This was early in our friendship, so we were still enamored with every gesture, smile, and word shared. Our conversations were effortless and flowed nicely. I genuinely enjoyed being in his presence. If I'm honest, however, I have to say I was equally excited about our destination. I really wanted donuts, and I wanted that big red "Hot and Ready" sign to be on.

As we pulled into the small, empty parking lot, we *were* greeted by the words "Hot and Ready," and both Jonathan and I silently cheered. This was going to work out perfectly. We bounced out of his red 1989 Toyota Corolla and casually strolled into the donut shop. We each ordered a few donuts, and when asked if they were "for here or to go," we chose "for here," but I added that I would like a half-dozen donuts to go. *This box will be for breakfast*, I thought to myself. I was being a responsible adult and thinking ahead. Jonathan laughed.

I don't remember how long we stayed, but I am sure I savored every moment, bite, and crumb. As we left, Jonathan carried my extra half-dozen donuts to the car. This is where things get a little fuzzy. Somewhere between our last bite and flirtatious smile inside the donut shop and arriving at my apartment, something terrible happened.

Jonathan decided he needed another donut.

He also decided he didn't need to buy one somewhere, because after all, I had six extra donuts. What he didn't know was that I had a well-thought-out plan for each one of them.

This, my friends, is what led to our first full-fledged argument. We didn't know it then, but we were fighting over something way bigger than donuts.

I guess you could say I won. He left hungry and free of the extra sugar he so angrily wanted. And though at the time I felt entitled, I would soon realize that getting my way didn't feel quite as filling as I would have liked.

Yes, I was selfish; I intended to eat every single morsel of those donuts myself. More important, however, was that we got a peek into our very souls. For a moment, I could see the real Jonathan, and he could see the real me, both of us imperfect, set in our ways, and feeling entitled.

Mistakes, history, expectations—these are three realities we all bring into our marriage relationship that can quickly crush our dreams.

Mistakes, history, expectations—these are three realities we all bring into our marriage relationship that can quickly crush our dreams. Everything about our evening had been great, but then these three realities came rushing in, quickly invading our relationship with toxicity.

This incident alone was not enough for too much pause. I accepted him, and he accepted me. We moved past the donuts and quickly into our futures from there. We accepted these realities without addressing their roots, in an attempt to make ourselves a new reality.

Jonathan

I still can't believe the strength Wynter had to deny me one of her "to go" donuts. It was a shock. As I grew up with a twin brother, nothing was ever "mine." Everything was shared. Obviously, this incident wasn't enough to stop me from pursuing her, however, because only a few months later, I proposed.

At that point in our relationship, she could do nothing wrong. She came into my life faster than anything I could have ever imagined. She was a godsend for sure. We had many more moments like we had in the donut story early and often in our dating and engagement life, and well into marriage, but we idealized our future together, somehow creating room for hope. It would have been difficult to imagine that our marriage could ever be on a rocky path.

Yet I found my face flat in the rocks right after the wedding. It was the week I had been living for—our honeymoon. Our dating life had been only eight months long, but our engagement had lasted a full year, and it had been full of raging hormones and strong emotions. We were married two weeks after our college graduation, and I was ready to start my life. I was ready to grow up. I was confident that our honeymoon would be the embodiment of everything I thought our marriage and future would become.

We faced many challenges throughout our engagement, some that we'll reference in the pages ahead, but I had little worry about our future. I had a great deal of confidence in my ability to make it work, to teach Wynter everything I knew about marriage and show her how it was done.

I thought I was ready. My parents' marriage had been a great example for me. I knew Scripture, and I had learned all about marriage in church and youth group. I had sung four years in our college's gospel choir. I was an Eagle Scout, and I had served most of our college years in our college's Army ROTC program. I was the walking, talking, Boy Scout motto—"Be Prepared."

That is, until I wasn't. You see, I was the epitome of what Jesus was talking about in Matthew 23:27:

> Woe to you, scribes and Pharisees, hypocrites! For you are like whitewashed tombs, which outwardly appear beautiful, but within are full of dead people's bones and all uncleanness.

Jesus was describing a group of men who looked good from the outside. They observed the law, and they wanted to make sure you knew it. Their faith was all about looking the part. They fasted and kept all the laws that would make people think they were pure, but inside they were greedy. They were selfish. They were hypocrites!

I was living the life of a hypocrite in many ways. This may sound harsh, but it's true. I kept my outer self nice and shiny. Just like whitewashed tombs in a cemetery, I looked "beautiful." I had the uncanny ability to make you think nothing but rosy thoughts, all the while harboring decay. I had impure thoughts and impure motives, and I took impure actions. But I covered it all up with accomplishment, success, and a "good guy" reputation.

Thank God Jesus died for hypocrites! The scariest thing about my hypocrisy wasn't that I was living a lie. After all, God forgives liars. The scariest thing was that my hypocrisy was allowing me to build up a false sense of security and worth. I put myself on a pedestal in my own eyes, which also allowed the expectation that God "owed" me in marriage. It went something like this in my mind:

I've been a morally good person. I've followed Jesus as best I can. Sure, I've made a few mistakes, but after asking for forgiveness, I've made up for them with more work. More accomplishment. God owes it to me to bless my life in marriage.

For years, I would build up two tabs. The first was what God owed me, and of course, God owed me the perfect marriage. The second was what my future wife would owe me. I thought, *Because I've been so perfect, she'll be honored to cater to my every need.*

Of course, I didn't vocalize these thoughts; a big part of me was blind to this reality. And now I can't help but laugh at my 23-year-old, naïve self who thought much more about himself than he thought about the woman God would give him, even in his ignorance and self-centeredness. I was about to experience one of the great shocks of my life!

We honeymooned in Puerto Vallarta, Mexico, on the west coast below the Baja Peninsula. Wynter's aunt and uncle, a young couple who mentored us in our dating and engaged days, gifted us this honeymoon at their beautiful time-share property. It was scenic. Picturesque. It was the perfect place for me to experience what I thought had been accruing for me, what was stored up in my mental marriage "IOU" box. I was ready to collect, and I just knew I was in for the week of my life.

Well, I was. It was just different from what I'd been expecting.

It turned out Wynter was just as much into the intimacy of conversation and mental rest as she was into any physical act. It took me many years to figure this out, but the combination of communication and rest (intimacy and a clear mind) leads to the latter. In my selfishness and immaturity, I had completely missed this lesson.

We had an amazing honeymoon. We rode horses through the mountains and zip lined through the forests. We swam and we sunbathed. But in addition to all that fun, that first week of marriage was a shocking reality check. I realized my marriage wasn't as much about me as I had thought.

And as if that shock weren't enough, I soon realized that thinking marriage would be mostly about me was only the first of multiple expectancies I had created in my mind. Every single one of them was the outcome of stored-up sin, false beliefs, and selfish expectations that shaped the early part of my marriage and led to so many disappointments, many of which I could have avoided through conversation.

I had brought these beliefs into marriage from a variety of mental gardens. You don't think about these gardens until you realize the rotten fruit they produce. From television, to my peer groups, to my role models, to my observations in life, I had filled my mind and heart with non-negotiable standards that are unobtainable and unreasonable for any spouse to meet.

This was week one, and that's all it took for me to realize that my growth as a husband and man would be impossible short of a miracle. That marriage wasn't about only me was the first and most eye-opening expectation crusher, but others were so serious and engrained that to this day they are difficult to overcome.

We have many similarities in our backgrounds. We both grew up in Christian homes. We both committed our lives to Jesus Christ at a young age. We both attended charismatic churches. We both enjoyed Brian McKnight, enough to go to a concert together a few months into dating. In those days I mostly focused on our similarities, paying little attention to our differences. I assumed my personality was strong enough to win her over to my side in any area of life where we differed. Because Wynter is a woman of few words, I didn't realize she had the same aspirations.

Boy, was I wrong, and so was she. We soon found our differences were quite different. I had little desire to become more like Wynter, and she had little desire to become more like me. Our perspective on donut availability was just the beginning of the challenges we would face, giving us a sneak peek into the life God was call-ing us into when we would finally say "I do." My stomach stayed empty after that argument about the donut, but little did I know how much further I would have to go in marriage.

Years later, we're still joking about those donuts, and every time we see that "Hot and Ready" sign, we're reminded of the beginning of our journey. It remains one of our favorite date nights! The story is hilarious, and if we were sitting face-to-face, you might have a similar story to tell.

> Can you imagine how many of us would follow
> through with marriage if we knew everything
> about each other from the beginning?

Like us, you likely began your journey with rose-colored glasses that minimized your differences. It wasn't necessarily a bad thing for us, and it wasn't necessarily a bad thing for you. Those glasses seem like common shades God gives each of us, allowing us to continue to put one foot in front of the other on our way to the aisle. Can you imagine how many of us would follow through with marriage if we knew everything about each other from the beginning? Don't get us wrong; we do believe that we should seek to know and understand each other as much as possible prior to marriage. Premarital coun-seling can help couples work through some of the factors that can affect their marriage. We went through premarital counseling with our pastor and it did help us begin to understand the differences we were bringing to the table. But what if we knew *all* our future spouse's quirks, sins, and mistakes? What if we knew their entire his-tory and all that they were bringing to the table hidden somewhere below the surface during our dating and engagement seasons? What if we could read all the expectations we had like a checklist? This would be quite paralyzing.

We thank God that He allowed us to see each other and our future through a set of rose-colored glasses. It's the only way He would get us into the same garden and ready for His pruning process. The pruning would begin early, and it continues, though the picture is much clearer and beautiful with each passing moment.

Your Turn

How did God's sovereign hand push your path together with your spouse's path? How has God orchestrated your story, and in what ways do you need to memorialize those God moments to recommit yourself to the journey?

Prayer

Father, from the very beginning of our days together, I've seen Your supreme hand at work. Even as I have focused on *me*, you have seen a *we*, and Your hand has continued to push me away from my own agenda and closer to Yours. Lord, I am in desperate need of Your help, because on my own, I continually get in the way of what You're doing. Help me focus on the fact that what You have started, You will continue, and that what I cannot accomplish on my own is Your specialty. Be gentle with me as You empty me of anything and everything that keeps me from pursuing the *we* You have in mind. In Jesus's name, amen.

2

Backgrounds

In our earliest days of dating, it was nearly impossible for us to think clearly about our differences, and rarely did we discuss them. Thankfully, we had our faith in Jesus in common, which, even then, we knew would be the glue that would bind. But we didn't realize how much glue it would take!

Though we came to it from different backgrounds, we both were committed to a similar view of marriage—a traditional view.

Jonathan

My story began with my parents, Garry and Miriam Pitts. They aren't a well-known couple. They haven't written any books, nor have they shared about their marriage publicly, at least not for the masses. But theirs is a story for the ages, all-inspiring for those who know it.

I was raised in a small Southern New Jersey town. When most people think of New Jersey, they don't think about the part I grew up in with cow pastures, cornfields, forests, and dark country roads.

I was a brownish biracial kid growing up in a brown-less town. My insecurities from being "different" were many, but all that was covered up by my talents, personal drive, and success. Thankfully, much stronger than even those was an understanding of truth based on God's Word, deposited deep inside my insecure soul.

My father, who is African-American, grew up in a single-parent home. He was raised by his mother, a strong and confident personality, along with her parents and a quiver full of aunts in an integrated and peaceful small town in Southern New Jersey. His father never married my grandmother, though he had a small role in my father's life. My father's upbringing was traditional and Baptist, much like the culture that surrounded him. He grew up amid the turbulent times of civil rights and integration. In his late teens, he made a commitment to Jesus Christ that began to shape everything about his future, including his marriage.

My mother was the granddaughter of German immigrants on both sides. Her one grandfather came to America to escape communism in Prussia before World War II, while her other grandparents came to America seeking opportunity in the sprawling Midwest. She grew up in a traditional German-American family, with her father a Lutheran Missouri Synod pastor of two small churches over a 50-plus-year career. With his faithful and talented wife by his side at the organ and in other various roles, he lived his entire lifetime in northwestern Iowan communities.

My father and mother met working at a residential music-farm school in their early twenties. For my dad, it was love at first sight, though their differences were enough for my mom to question the likelihood of a bright future. Yet their love for music and God's providential hand created a long-distance romance. My father's intentions grew into a relentless pursuit that eventually ended in victory against all odds; the beliefs about interracial marriage in the 1970s were a great barrier.

Their lives could not have looked any more different from the world's perspective, but the world left out one thing my parents held on to with tenacity—the purposes of God. They understood something few in our day choose to even consider. They believed and held on to the fact that passion and fullness in marriage come when a couple understands that God's purpose in marriage is far greater than the sum of two people's lives.

Garry and Miriam knew that 1 + 1 had a sum much greater than 2 in the economy of God. They trusted that their union would add up to God's purposes being fulfilled in their lives, as well as in the lives of those He would influence through them, starting with their children, moving on to their grandchildren, and making an impact on generations to come.

They believed Genesis 2:24: "A man shall leave his father and mother and be joined to his wife, and they shall become one flesh" (NKJV). And I was the direct beneficiary.

My mom had no earthly idea God would pull her out of a very white Midwest culture and plop her into the arms of a Black man in the Northeast. Together they would die to the thoughts, concerns, worries, and whispers of others about their interracial marriage. They died at that marriage altar, and they died consistently afterward, putting the needs of the other before their own.

The most vivid childhood memories I have of my parents are images of them giving, not taking. My dad gave up his time and energy to provide for my mom, my siblings, and me. He typically worked two full-time jobs to make ends meet in a difficult 1980s economy, but he never complained and owned his responsibility. And I remember my mom giving up her expectations of what life "should" be like to fulfill the purpose God had given them. She wanted to be an artist and a writer. She liked working with print media. And though she didn't necessarily want children, God changed her heart. She ended up with five children and has lived a life of selfless service in marriage and parenting, giving up her career to prioritize our home. I watched her take care of my dad, who had epileptic seizures, in my childhood. Even as a young man, I knew there were other things that she wanted to do, but she found contentment in God's calling on her life. Their road wasn't easy in those early days, and my parents spoke often of their total reliance on the Lord. They were a team in their desperation for God to show up. I have few memories of disappointment and mostly memories of perseverance and lessons learned as they were obedient to their calling.

My ideas about marriage were greatly shaped by the one I saw in front of me. My parents were models who gave me confidence that my marriage would make it regardless of what came. But I had never experienced, valued, or understood the level of work required for them to succeed. That would come only with time and my own experience. I couldn't fully appreciate the level of commitment, sacrifice, and sheer grit it took them to overcome the circumstances, disappointments, and setbacks inevitable in life to thrive.

If you were to ask Garry and Miriam Pitts about their several decades of marriage, though, they would tell you it wasn't their sheer grit and determination that gave them success. Instead, they would share about the mystery of God's kindness and their love and commitment to Jesus Christ. They would speak much of the Lord's pruning process in their lives that led to long-term faithfulness full of purpose, passion, and fulfillment, and their five children and 13 (and counting) grandchildren, as well as a steadfast love and joy that continue today.

Wynter

I am a city girl. I was born and raised in Baltimore, Maryland. You may not know my neighborhood by name, but you've likely seen it on cable news over the past few years because of the riots. Or you could have seen it on the hit HBO shows *The Wire* or *The Corner*. While Maryland is known for its crabs, Baltimore is known for its drugs, gangs, and endless streets of row homes filled with poverty-stricken people. I'll never forget the first time my daughters saw the block of row homes on the street where I lived. "Wow, Mommy, your house was huge," my oldest daughter said, not realizing our home was only one small fraction of our block's sea of entirely attached homes.

My home was a corner unit. Opposite my corner was a corner store. Out my bedroom window, I daily watched people go in and out of that store buying all manner of unhealthy food options while simultaneously watching others do business with the local drug dealers on the sidewalks. I watched them buy, and I have numerous memories of watching others use.

While Jonathan grew up surrounded by fields of corn and compost piles, I played in a cement backyard, one of the things Jonathan likes to bring up often when we're discussing our different backgrounds with someone. The first time Jonathan saw this part of Baltimore, he couldn't get over the sight of thousands of city blocks and fenced-in areas of cracked concrete. For me, however, nothing about my rocky play area was abnormal. It was perfect for riding my bike in small circles around the metal pole we used for drying clothes. If you've never experienced a cement backyard, I am so sorry to tell you, but you have never witnessed true city living.

My city living is just a small piece of the package I carried into marriage. Given the overwhelming joblessness, poverty, and availability of cheap highs in Baltimore, many families in my neighborhood experienced a life full of poverty, drug abuse, and fatherlessness, mine not much different.

Although my parents married and were young and happy newlyweds, my father's decision to experiment with drugs early on led him down a long and destructive road of drug abuse. His addiction prevented him from having any role in my childhood. His decisions and their outcomes, including their eventual divorce, left my mother overwhelmed and desperate to figure out how to raise two children on her own.

Thankfully, hope exists in despair. My father's brother was the first person to introduce my mother to an understanding of a personal relationship with Christ, planting seeds of hope. Christ became her lifeline in an impossible circumstance.

My mother often tells the story of taking her first faith step when she was eight months pregnant with me and my brother was five years old. She was living with and in my father's addiction, and she was smack in the middle of some of the hardest days of her life. The details are hard to unpack, but in this place of desperation, Christ swooped her off her feet. Although she didn't grow up in a Christian home, her mother (my grandmother) had recently started attending a church and invited my mother to go with her. Thankfully, she never stopped going, and to this day she attends this same church!

There, she found people who accepted her, held her up in her weakest moments, and loved her right into the arms of her Savior. With me in her belly, she began her personal relationship with Christ. I think it's so great that I get to say, "I've been going to church since before I was born!" The example she set before me when I was a little girl has greatly affected all areas of my life, and it became the foundation of my own personal relationship with Jesus.

When I was only one year old, we moved into a three-bedroom house with my grandmother, along with an aunt and two female cousins. My mother and grandmother, two God-fearing women, had a massive influence on my life. I lived with them until I left for college at the age of 18. My mother and grandmother would live out, quite literally, the prophecy of Isaiah 54:5:

> For your Maker is your husband, the LORD of hosts is
> his name; and the Holy One of Israel is your Redeemer,
> the God of the whole earth he is called.

God was their husband, and He would be my father, but I grew up in a home full of and led by women. My brother was there, but he was being raised by them too. From my perspective, this way of life had some benefits. Routine discipline wasn't super high on my mother and grandmother's radar, and because life was already so tough, they went out of their way to make sure I didn't notice the difference. But as you can imagine, this environment had its challenges. The women in my home did it all. They were the homemakers, breadwinners (the little bread we had), disciplinarians, and spiritual leaders. Simply put, for 18 years, the wisdom, advice, and conversations that played on repeat in my ear were in the female voice and from the female perspective. I simply did not see, hear, or know the other side of the aisle very well.

Marriage, for me, was seen only from a distance. Sure, I had aunts and uncles who were married, and my grandparents on my father's side stand out as spiritual giants in marriage, remaining married for over 50 years before my grandmother passed away. But seeing, hearing, noticing, and witnessing marriage daily and with proximity just wasn't available.

Thankfully, my home was full of hope and rooted in Christ.

Despite the many things we lacked, my mother's and my grandmother's faith in Christ drove their actions. They relied on and rested in Christ as they raised my brother, Sean, and me. They did their best to teach me God's Word and show me what it meant to live as His daughter. They gave me a God-size vision for what I should expect in life, including expectations for a godly man, but vision and experience are different.

Despite the hardships she's endured, my mother has shown me so much about what a Christlike life should look like. She has always been one of the most gentle, humble, and selfless people I know. I have vivid memories of her giving strangers on the street rides, food, and even pieces of clothing off her back! As a little girl and even teen, I could never wrap my mind around this type of kindness and generosity, especially from someone who in the eyes of many had nothing to offer. All these examples stood out, but her ability to forgive and love my father, despite the harm he did our family, stands out as a true act of heroism. I could see no bitterness, no resentment, no anger in her—only compassion. I resented it for many years, but I came to realize it was her only choice as she followed her new Savior, who had been so forgiving and compassionate to her.

My mother remarried my freshman year of college, and I cannot fully express how grateful I am to have witnessed her journey of becoming a wife. Even though I was no longer living under the same roof, I'm grateful that God gave me a glimpse of what it looks like when a woman, fully in love with Him, decides to fully love and commit herself to another. My mother is not perfect, but her love for Christ is strong, and that has always been undeniable to those around her, including me. Looking back now, although I didn't see it practically lived out with a husband, I pulled more from her that would benefit me in my marriage relationship than I would know until years later.

Now one of the greatest joys I have in life is watching her interact with her husband, my brother and me, our spouses, and her seven grandchildren. Her faithful struggle and prayers to God have been met with His richest blessings, and they stand as witness to a watching world of both what a life submitted to God can look like and the power of redemption.

Each of our families faced many challenges—racial differences, setbacks, health scares, loss, and more. But in each case, they gave us a vision for life that was broad and hopeful. Even in the difficulties, their lives reminded us to look beyond.

Our families understood that the strength of their relationship and commitment to one another, over and above their individual and momentary needs, trumped their emotions, feelings, temptations, and temporary happiness. They were confident in Philippians 1:6, which says, "He who began a good work in you will perfect it until the day of Christ Jesus" (NASB).

We came from significantly different backgrounds and different family makeups. Those differences have absolutely come with challenges and misunderstandings. Thankfully, there was one common denominator—a commitment and dedication to following Jesus Christ.

In Matthew 16:24, "Jesus told his disciples, 'If anyone would come after me, let him deny himself and take up his cross and follow me.'"

Following Jesus is a process that has allowed us to think about and see ourselves less so we can see each other more.

> Something beautiful happens when you begin
> to see the beauty in your spouse.

Something beautiful happens when you begin to see the beauty in your spouse, when you no longer see their differences as threats to your well-being, but as enhancements to your life, and when you begin to see their story as a work of God and a perfect picture of grace.

In our marriages, God is calling each of us to imitate Him—to follow Jesus—in all His grace, mercy, and compassion.

He looks at each of us, seeing the entirety of our background—the good, bad, and ugly—and still offers us hope and ultimately redemption as we trust in Him.

Your Turn

You've brought your own background and history to where you are. You've brought some good and some not so good. Take some time to examine your past. What has God given you that will benefit your marriage as you move forward? What have you brought in that might need to go?

Prayer

Lord, I thank You for the characteristics and traits

You've graciously given me that will benefit my marriage as I journey on. I thank You for everything I've been through that has made me who I am. I submit all of who I am to You. Use the good, the bad, and the ugly to shape my marriage into the masterpiece You have in mind, and help me remember that there is no part of my life and background You cannot use as I submit to Your process. In Jesus's name, amen.

3

God's Kingdom Purposes

Visions for marriage vary. Some people marry for happiness. Their pursuit is for individual satisfaction, and it's all about what they are being offered by their spouse. When that expectation stops being fed, however, they become dissatisfied at best and begin looking elsewhere at worst.

Others marry in pursuit of materialistic gain. This version can present itself as the American dream. You know, shiny diamond, comfortable house, white picket fence, 2.5 kids, and a bank account that gives you all the worldly success you can dream of.

Still others marry for escape. They believe if they can change their reality by creating a new one, they can move beyond their past. But then they discover their past walked right in the front door with them.

> Our marriages are about building God's kingdom.

From a gospel perspective there is only one motive for marriage.

It comes from the author of marriage Himself, God. Simply put, the kingdom is better when we're together—we, meaning us and you. Our marriages are about building God's kingdom.

The kingdom of God is bigger than us, and it's bigger than you. It includes us, but the purpose of a marriage union goes well beyond two individuals.

Let us explain.

God's vision for marriage starts in Genesis, where He gives us a clear snapshot of a marriage in Adam and Eve. In the first few chapters of Genesis, God recorded an overview of what marriage and family were to be for the entire world. We suggest reading these few chapters, but we'll pull out a few key highlights.

God's vision of marriage had multiple purposes, all with His kingdom in mind. After making Eve and declaring that Adam and Eve would be co-laborers in the Garden of Eden, God makes a statement: "A man shall leave his father and mother and be joined to his wife, and they shall become one flesh" (Genesis 2:24 NKJV).

Although they were individuals in the relationship, Adam and Eve were given the command to live as a single unit. God intentionally joined them together with a specific purpose: They were to serve each other, a purpose greater than serving themselves. Along with that, God wanted them to manage children and His creation.

In Genesis 1:28 we're told, "God blessed them and said to them, 'Be fruitful and increase in number; fill the earth and subdue it'" (NIV).

"Be fruitful." That's a simple way to say "reproduce," yes? Yes, of course, but it's a little deeper than that, because the verse before this one, Genesis 1:27, says, "God created mankind in his own image, in the image of God he created them; male and female he created them" (NIV).

Two things were being reproduced and multiplied. The first was children, and the second was the image of God.

This is beautiful imagery, and it's potent with implication. Many Scriptures give us more specificity for how this would work, and some of it we'll cover as we go further in the book. But skipping over an exhaustive study of these Scriptures, we should still easily take away three concepts in terms of purpose for marriage:

- relational oneness
- reproducing ourselves
- nurturing the image of God

What does all this have to do with all of us?

Let's start with oneness. The simplest, one-word definition of oneness and a term that will help us grab the concept is "unity." If unity is encapsulated in our vision, then that picture should directly affect how we think and act in marriage and toward our spouses. If you asked the average person on the street what they wanted most in marriage, they would likely say happiness. Well, happiness is a result and byproduct of something else. It's a state of mind based on circumstances. We would argue that the something else that gives us true happiness is fulfilling the purposes of God, starting with unity in our marriages—oneness.

If we understand oneness, then happiness can result, but pursuing happiness doesn't necessarily bring about oneness. In fact, pursuing happiness might lead us away from oneness because happiness can be a fleeting and ever-moving target motivated by self-interests. But more on that later.

Second, if reproducing ourselves is a part of God's vision for our marriages, then that should also have an impact on our journeys. Obviously, the first thought that comes to mind when we hear "reproduce yourself" is childbirth, but we won't argue that parenting must be in every married couple's future. Regardless, the thought of reproduction should have us thinking about the reasons God commanded us to reproduce in the first place. Ask yourself, *Can I reproduce the character, qualities, and gifts God has given me in those He has put in my path, biologically related or not?*

For us, the greatest opportunity to reproduce ourselves is in our four daughters. They are beautiful walking, talking, imitating pictures of our unity, and we have little doubt that they are the fruit of our labor. We have had, however, multiple opportunities to reproduce ourselves beyond our children. From the afterschool programs we've served in, to our nieces, nephews, neighbors, and friends, God has given us amazing opportunities to share in the reproduction of our God-given gifts, expertise, and talents. He has given us the opportunity to shape employees and a myriad of others who all serve in the collective effort of managing His creation.

Every time you reproduce a child or a trait in someone else on this earth as a part of your unified marriage, you are fulfilling God's vision and participating in His plan.

That leads us to the greatest and most rewarding purpose of marriage—the nurturing of God's image. We'll ask you one question in regard to your marriage and your spouse: How are you loving and nurturing God's image in those around you? You might answer that you're investing in your biological children, or in adoption, or in sharing your faith, or in mentoring someone. In any case, God is calling each of us as believers in Jesus Christ to nurture His image and call every person into a deeper relationship with Him through Jesus Christ.

Having each of our daughters and watching them grow has been the ultimate eye-opener in our understanding that God's purpose for our marriage is really all about Him. Each of our daughters has been uniquely handcrafted by God, and according to the Bible, has His unique fingerprint on her life. We love how the writer of Acts expresses this fact:

> The God who made the world and everything in it, being Lord of heaven and earth, does not live in temples made by man, nor is he served by human hands, as though he needed anything, since he himself gives to all mankind life and breath and everything. And he made from one man every nation of mankind to live on all the face of the earth, having determined allotted periods and the boundaries of their dwelling place, that they should seek God, and perhaps feel their way toward him and find him. Yet he is actually not far from each one of us, for "In him we live and move and have our being"; as even some of your own poets have said, "For we are indeed his offspring" (Acts 17:24-28).

Every one of us is God's offspring, and we can participate in the cultivation of His image.

Every one of us is God's offspring, and we can participate in the cultivation of His image. Reproducing ourselves and the image of God has its basis in parenting, but it includes fostering and a myriad of other good works that give others an opportunity to know Jesus Christ. Ultimately, nurturing God's image in each other is a work we all get to participate in. It starts when we accept Jesus Christ as creator and perfecter and open our lives to His refining process.

First Thessalonians 5:23 says, "The very God of peace sanctify you wholly; and I pray God your whole spirit and soul and body be preserved blameless unto the coming of our Lord Jesus Christ" (KJV).

We'd like to tell you the vision we brought into marriage was picture perfect. We wish we could say that, having grown up with an understanding of God's commands, we absorbed all that is good within them. It would be nice to share that we took in everything we learned from our parents and implemented their strategies into our marriage—their stick-to-itiveness, their deference to each other, their willingness to forgive despite what the other had done. Unfortunately, we brought some things in that would leave only on the other side of trials, experience, and a willingness to humble ourselves.

Jonathan

I knew the vision. I knew it well. I watched it lived out in my father's life. I watched him pour out his life for my mother. I watched his daily sacrifices. But instead of walking in his ways, I came into my marriage trying to fulfill my own happiness. I wouldn't have told you that. But if you had watched my life closely, you would have noticed.

Instead of taking the time to care for Wynter's needs, I much preferred to serve my own. I'd go to the gym without a thought of what Wynter needed. In conversations, I would belabor my points rather than listen to her perspective. In arguments, I would much prefer to completely inundate Wynter with my winsome words and personality, as if that's all she needed in her life. I needed to grow, and that was no doubt easy for others to see. To be honest, I still need to grow.

Wynter

When Jonathan and I got married, we had a five-year plan, and it was simple. We would use the first five years of our marriage to concentrate on saving, traveling, building careers, and all aspects of growing together. I am not going to debate whether we all enter marriage as two full beings or two incomplete halves. I'll leave that for the experts in other books. I will simply say that when Jonathan and I married at 23, we had a lot of growing up to do, and we didn't even realize it.

Honestly, I thought I knew what I was doing. In my mind, being a wife wasn't that complicated, and my life was destined to be better because it was my husband's role to be sure of it.

Obviously, it's easy to see how ridiculous a thought it was, but I'm positive I'm not the only woman who has entered marriage expecting her husband to fix it. In my case, the "it" was 20-plus years of brokenness from not experiencing the love of an earthly father. I was counting on Jonathan to mend my broken heart, buy me a new car, and read my mind so he could surprise me daily with how deeply he understood and knew the true me.

I may have never said these exact words, but I did treat marriage like a lamp I could rub so out would pop my genie (Jonathan) to grant my wish instantly and adhere to my every command. You may be wondering where on earth I got my vision of a husband, so I'll tell you: It's my grandmother's fault!

Not really, but she does play a part.

You see, if I were to list my top three childhood friends, my grandmother would quite possibly be in the number one space. I was only one year old when my mother and father divorced, and we moved into my grandmother's house. I'll take this a step further and let you know that I literally moved in with my grandmother, meaning, she and I became roommates. I shared a room and bed with her until I was ten. Saying we were extremely close almost feels like an understatement. My mother worked a good amount and was trying to rebuild her life after my father's addictions shattered her world. Don't get me wrong; she was very much involved in my life, and I never once doubted her love for me, but during those years I spent the majority of my time with my grandmother, also known as Mama.

Every night before bed, Mama and I watched a few of her favorite shows. Some nights we watched one of her favorite movies. Eventually her favorites became my favorites, and I still love a good, sappy, maybe even corny love story. That started with Julia Roberts and Richard Gere. That's right, one of our favorite movies to watch was *Pretty Woman*. If you're thinking, *That's totally inappropriate for a little girl to watch*, you are correct. My grandmother didn't mean any harm, though, and, well, it just was what it was, folks!

In the movie, Julia Roberts plays a beautiful young woman who has fallen into a pretty unrespectable lifestyle, and she just can't seem to catch a break in life. Enter Richard Gere, playing a handsome, wealthy businessman. He hires Julia's character to keep him company for a week in Los Angeles while he's there for business. His presence changes everything for her. He leaves her wads of cash to shop and pay bills, and he even moves her into his hotel penthouse! When people mistreat her, he defends her and fixes everything broken. All in the same week, he surprises her with fancy dates, new dresses, shoeless strolls through green grass, and playing in water fountains! By the end of the movie, Julia's character is a new woman, all because she's fallen in love. Richard Gere's character is her genie in a bottle, and when I was at a very young and impressionable age, this fantasy became the reality on which I based my future.

Now, while nothing is wrong with a good love story in and of itself, for a fatherless, ten-year-old girl, this one was nothing short of dangerous. Basing my standards for a man on scripted messages in perfectly orchestrated scenes was unhealthy, and obviously unfair to Jonathan.

Before Jonathan, no man came close to making me feel the way Richard made Julia feel, so I automatically knew none of them was the one for me. However, something felt different about Jonathan from the start. He cared about me in a way that made me come to expect it.

His presence seemed to fix everything, and the more he made me smile, the more I expected him to. Though Richard Gere's character wasn't close to being Jesus, many of the characteristics in his life were Christlike. Think about it: selfless love, passionate pursuit, seeing beyond her past, and a willingness to forgive. Obviously, this illustration breaks down, but a lot of what I saw in Gere's character was God honoring. I now realize the danger in mistaking and recognizing the Christlike actions of man for those of Christ Himself. Let me explain.

Jonathan loves Jesus, and that love drives his actions and care for others. My heart was drawn to this type of love; I had been longing for it. No matter how hard Jonathan tried to be Christ to me, the parts of my heart that needed to be touched could be reached only by Jesus. Until I realized this, the unfair, unrealistic, and selfish expectations I put on my husband left him feeling like a failure, while I continued to demand he step up to the plate and fix my unsatisfied heart.

I'm sure you see the problem here, but for so long I did not. Only God could begin to reveal to me the love my heart longed for. Only God could help me understand His love was what I needed. I couldn't assume my husband was a replacement for the earthly father I'd missed.

We needed to grow. We needed a standard. We knew we wouldn't be happy until we started this journey.

We're guessing since you're reading this book, you're interested in moving toward God's plan for your life. You have your own "Richard Gere"—someone you've assumed can fix your life—and your own misperceptions that need to be righted. You aren't the type of person who's content with who you are, and you're desperate to find more of who God created you to be. You know your life can go in only two directions—up a path toward vivacity and flourishing, or in a downward spiral, quick or belabored, toward decay and poverty. You are pursuing vivacity and flourishing. You are interested in a better life! But a question consistently nags you: *How do I get there?*

We also assume you're trying desperately to find out how you can move toward God's vision for your marriage—one that lines up with His purposes. You want to know how your marriage can become all God intends it to be. Beyond that, we're assuming you're interested in being more than a good spouse. You're desperate to become a great spouse. You realize that just like your personal life, your marriage will tend toward one of two directions—up a path toward vivacity and flourishing, or in a downward spiral, quick or belabored, toward decay and poverty. We're certain you're interested in the best marriage! But the same nagging question comes with this line of thinking: *How do I get there?*

Ask the most seasoned married couples if they have "arrived," and the most mature and most godly will say, "We never arrive."

Achieving success in individual growth or a godly marriage is more difficult than we want to hear in our natural state. That's because in both cases, the answer is beyond anything we can muster on our own. "Getting there" in personal growth and in marriage is beyond us. It's honestly otherworldly. Ask the most seasoned married couples if they have "arrived," and the most mature and most godly will say, "We never arrive."

This may sound like a minor point, but we promise you it's major. Think about it. If you have the mind-set that you're supposed to arrive in marriage, what happens if you never do? What happens if you experience more bumps in the road and more detours than you were prepared to face?

But on the other hand, if you have the mind-set that your marriage is a journey that will be full of bumps, detours, and any manner of dangerous turns, how will that change your perspective when the tough times come and disappointment sets in?

We've been married long enough to know that our journey is just getting started. Our bumps started early and return often, and the detours happen much more often than we ever would have volunteered to tackle. In this process, we've found that marriage isn't a destination where we can arrive, but a continual journey that requires a specific mind-set and a heart toward execution. The challenge comes when the reality hits that both the mind-set and the heart required don't fit within our human bodies.

Can you be a great husband or wife on your own and in your own strength? Well, the answer to that question depends on who is judging. We're not saying you can't be great in certain areas of your life and certain areas of your marriage. We're guessing parts of you scream with gifting and skill. But we are saying that, without some sort of supernatural help, you're going to routinely fall short in other areas.

To grow as a person or to grow in your marriage, a standard is required. If you don't have a standard, you can't measure your growth. You'll point aimlessly and with no target. You'll meander helplessly with a nebulous destination.

In writing this book, we unashamedly point to a singular set of standards that have stood the test of time and continue to show results for all who dare trust their guidance to the end. That set of standards is the Word of God, the Bible.

God's Word as written in Genesis through Revelation gives us a wealth of wisdom, instruction, and guidance on the topic of marriage and a clear path for any man or woman seeking the best marriage.

But God doesn't ask us to do this alone. His Word points us in the right direction, and He gives us His help. We need only to ask.

Your Turn

In what ways are you pursuing God's purpose for your marriage?

In what ways have you preferred to pursue your own purpose? How can you change today to put God's purpose in front of your own?

Prayer

God, more often than not, I have put my preferences and purpose in front of Yours in my marriage. I have cared far too much about accomplishing what I've wanted and too little about what You've asked of me. May You begin to shape and mold my mind and heart to be more like Yours. And may I begin to measure my success in marriage against Your standard, not my feelings. Lord, bring Your supernatural vivacity and flourishing into my marriage as I give myself to You and allow You to point out needed change. In Jesus's name, amen.

4

Live Shot

Jonathan

If you had asked me if I was ready to walk the aisle before our wedding day, I would have quickly and confidently told you yes. With absolutely no reserve, I would have shared all the ways God had prepared me for marriage. In my own mind, I was an ideal candidate for a husband.

I could have checked a lot of boxes that would put me in the "righteous boy" category. From the outside, I looked the part. I was respectful. I knew the right things to say to anyone asking. I had little on my resume that would give anyone pause.

I had a lot going for me. I was a "good Christian." As mentioned before, I sang in the gospel choir. I was academically gifted. I was a high-ranking leader within my ROTC program at my college, and I maintained a reputation in the marketplace that commanded respect.

I was a hard worker, and it showed in most every area of my life. I maintained a steady, almost full-time job during my junior and senior years, while always carrying more than a typical semester's worth of credits at a time.

I excelled. Of course, I did. That's what I wanted. That was my aim and highest goal. And if I'm being honest, I have to say that the fear of being exposed as something other than "most likely to succeed" was my greatest fear.

I'm not exactly sure where this fear came from, but I suppose it came from growing up a mixed-race boy, never feeling like I fit in. At least that's what I would share if I was sitting down with a counselor asking me the root issues in my life.

So instead of trying to fit in, I pushed myself to the top, daily. It didn't matter whether it was sports, work, or extracurricular activities. I wanted to be pictured at the top of the class. I didn't want to be seen or remembered as anything less than the best.

Frankly, it worked with most people and in most scenarios. That's because most people are looking at your life as a snapshot. They never spend enough time with you to see the real you. They see only what you allow them to see.

Keeping up your image is easy to do in a snapshot, because you have to hold your pose for only a split second.

Keeping up your image is easy to do in a snapshot, because you have to hold your pose for only a split second. Many of us learn to hold the pose at just the right time. Once the picture is taken, we go back to our normal selves.

Then a beautiful young woman with much less of an image issue began to expose the rest of the film in my life.

If you walked into our home, you'd see that beautifully framed, black-and-white wedding photo we wrote about earlier sitting on our fireplace mantel. In every home we've owned, that photo has been in a common space, reminding us of a day we remain grateful for, with fond memories stored.

Wynter was born with a million-dollar smile, and she passed it on to each of our four daughters. All five of them have large, beautifully straight teeth, with just the right lip size and posture to support an entire photo. Our wedding photo is proof of that reality in Wynter.

Wynter is leaning into my chest, her head snuggled into my neck, her left arm wrapped around my side, and her right arm grabbing my body just under my shoulders. My chin is pressed into her nose, and though her eyes aren't visible, you can see joy in her entire face. I'm looking down at her with awe and wonder, with one arm clasping her left arm and the other placed gently on her back.

It's a beautiful picture. It's a picture for the ages. Did I mention my hair looks perfect? I kid, but it does!

Yet it's a snapshot. It's a very good snapshot, but a snapshot nonetheless.

Wynter

In my mind, our wedding day was close to picture perfect. I didn't grow up collecting wedding dress ideas or dreaming of floral arrangements, but somehow as Jonathan and I spent our senior year in college planning a wedding, all the details seemed to fall into the right places. Just about every weekend, we hopped into the car and made the 90-minute drive from Philadelphia to Baltimore to meet with bakers, venue managers, musicians, and designers. I had (and I still have) a huge baby-blue notebook full of black-and-white website printouts, emails, time lines, budgets, and receipts. I'm not sure

I've managed to be this organized since, yet somehow during that time it just felt natural.

We married on a Friday evening at a mansion right outside of Baltimore City. I use the term *mansion* loosely, because the place wasn't that large or extravagant. But it was a gorgeous property and a perfect venue for the intimate ceremony and reception we'd envisioned. We married on a Friday evening because it allowed for a little more room in our budget. (There's a nice tip for any engaged couples who find themselves reading this book!)

I remember waking up the morning of the wedding and feeling at total peace. It wasn't because Jonathan and I didn't have any bumps along the way to the altar, because we definitely did. Yet somehow, despite the arguments, misunderstandings, and areas of concern, I woke up with a confidence that moving forward with marriage was part of God's plan for our lives.

I can honestly say I wouldn't do many things differently. It was a beautiful day, and it remains one of my most cherished memories.

When I look at the photographs from our wedding, however, I always feel a little ache in my heart. The one thing I would change is our photographer. The photos captured don't give justice to the moments we experienced. Whenever I look at our album with our girls, I find myself filling in the blanks and retelling the moments leading up to the images that made their way into the photo book.

I say things like, "Oh, I remember what song we were dancing to!" or "Oh, that's a funny picture, but Poppi was telling a joke, and that's why Daddy's face looks like that!"

Let's just say our photographer went for more of the candid shots; however, one staged photo was worth framing because he managed to capture my head tilting just the perfect angle to give the impression that I was resting on my new husband's chest. That's the one we framed to place on our fireplace mantel, the one Jonathan described for you.

Even with that image, I can recall so much more to the story.

Moments before that photo was taken, Jonathan and I were having a mild disagreement. I don't remember over what, but I remember that it happened. Yet somehow, what was captured is beautiful.

Despite my disappointment in our photographer's ability to, in most cases, capture perfect images, I've come to realize that the images we could print aren't what made our day special. The moments leading up to that final image are what made the first day of our forever one to cherish—the good, bad, and funny.

> In marriage, it's easy to focus most of our time on trying to capture the perfect picture, but it's the day-in and day-out moments we need to capture and remember.

In marriage, it's easy to focus most of our time on trying to capture the perfect picture, but it's the day-in and day-out moments we need to capture and remember.

One of my favorite features on updated smartphones is the ability to capture a "live shot." I'll explain what that is in case you're not familiar with it. A live shot lets you see, along with the final image you've taken, the milliseconds of movements made getting your subject into the final position. As you can imagine, these images can be hilarious. With a selfie, it's as if you smiled in slow motion, so not only is the image when both your lips were wrapped perfectly around your teeth captured, but also every movement your bottom lip made to get into position. Live shots give me a new appreciation for the imperfect.

They are a reminder that, in our marriages, there is no perfect picture. Marriage is a combination of imperfect movements that, when caught at the right millisecond, manage to create something lovely. Perfect pictures—or in the case of our wedding photos, imperfect pictures—beg for a story to be told.

Here's a bit more of our live shot in fast-forward.

In five years, we successfully birthed four children and moved our family across the country. Our only plan was to raise our children in the Lord…on one income!

Startling and unplanned announcements can pretty much sum up the road my husband journeyed on for our first ten years together. We had change after change, ups and downs, and a few zigzags along the way. But in the middle of our story is one reality: Any spiritual maturity, as a couple, came as a learning experience amid unstable and seemingly chaotic circumstances.

Coincidence? I think not.

At some point your circumstances, environment, or day-to-day situation will inevitability change, but God's plan and purpose do not.

Your marriage might not have had as much drastic change as mine has had, or maybe your story makes mine look like a cake walk, but the lesson remains the same. At some point your circumstances, environment, or day-to-day situation will inevitability change, but God's plan and purpose do not. Amid uncertainty and instability, God has a way of making His way feel right as we choose to obey and follow the call He has placed on our lives. If Christ is at the center of our marriages, our job is not to create a comfortable life, but to develop a life that is securely grounded, despite uncomfortable circumstances.

Unfortunately, in marriage we often assume a false sense of ownership, believing that taking the hand of the person who is our best friend, lifelong partner, and spouse will lead us into a life of stability and prediction. A life of happily ever afters. Before we get to the ever afters, however, we see unforeseen right nows, like changing environments, shifting dynamics, and brand-new realities. They inevitability lead us to forks in the road. When life makes us face-to-face with instability, we must choose to find security in the creator of our destiny, Christ.

Proverbs 3:5-6 says, "Trust in the LORD with all your heart, and do not lean on your own understanding. In all your ways acknowledge him, and he will make straight your paths."

Recently, I found myself on the other end of the phone as a dear friend and mentor made a big announcement: "I am 42, I am pregnant, and my husband is starting a new business."

She was unexpectedly having a fourth child just as her husband had started off on a great adventure of entrepreneurial risk. To complicate things further, I recalled a few conversations from weeks earlier about her joining her husband in this new endeavor. It seemed then that she was content to move into a new season, and I knew a new baby was not a part of her plan.

I remained silent because I was waiting for my cue to step in. I was ready to tell her it was going to be okay. I was going to be the mature one—you know, comfort her amid her uncertainty. After all, isn't that what friends do?

We talked for a while about the change this was going to cause for her family's future plans. To my astonishment, she ended our conversation with a simple, yet profound statement:

"Clearly God is in this. It's going to work out. What else can I say?

God has ordained these things to happen. These are His plans, and He promises to keep us through it. He sees. He knows. He cares."

I was in awe. This type of trust doesn't come easily or overnight. It cannot be earned or forced. It's the result of an intentional, daily commitment to submitting ourselves, our plans, and our personal comfort to the authority of God.

I am grateful for a God who provides examples and confirmation through the wisdom of others, and even more so through His Word!

Consider Abram and Sarai having to announce to the entire family that they were to pack up and leave because God told them to travel to an unknown place He would show them (Genesis 12). They had to stabilize their hearts and move, believing God was in control.

Or how about when Noah told his family God had commanded him to build an ark because it was going to rain, and then live in it as He prescribed (Genesis 6)? His trust was amazing, but have you ever considered the trust his family displayed in God to go along with that? It worked out for them! Noah, his wife, and his children chose to live in obedience. They built the ark and submitted to the plan. It did rain, and they survived the flood.

What about Job, who was determined to trust God even when his spouse did not (Job 2)? He was convinced he needed to trust the Lord and accept adversity as well as good. Job made a firm commitment to act as if he could lean on the character of God, even when his emotions disagreed.

Let's not forget the most amazing trust in the Lord of all. Mary, a teenager, had to announce to Joseph, her fiancé, and to their families that she was pregnant, and that the father was God (Luke 1). Individually, Mary and Joseph chose to shift their focus from fear to trusting God's plan, despite the rumors and mocking surely circulating.

What announcements are you facing? A change in parental status, a big move, an illness, or even a loss?

In what ways can you shift your focus?

How can you stabilize your heart and give God control over your circumstances?

Are you committed to trusting in who God is, despite what you see and what you don't understand?

And like Noah, are you committed to obedience?

Stability can be defined as resistance to change. But when I think of godly marriages, this connotation does not come to mind.

On the other hand, security can be defined as freedom from danger or well-founded confidence.

Bingo.

> God doesn't promise us stability; however,
> submission to His will promises security,
> in our marriages and in our lives.

God calls us to secure marriages that are constantly evolving, changing, and growing as we navigate through the unforeseen circumstances in life. God doesn't promise us stability; however, submission to His will promises security, in our marriages and in our lives.

Marriage is not a snapshot. It's a live shot. Although for most of our youthful lives we tend to skip from one snapshot to

another—from one relationship to another, never allowing someone to see us for who we really are—marriage is the beginning of one
live shot after another. Yes, you will have opportunities to capture
a snapshot, and those moments are still important. But marriage is
living and active. It opens the door for full exposure and vulnerability that never quite existed in your life before.

To many of us, the thought of this kind of exposure feels threat-
ening and awkward, a barrier to our ability to live from one snapshot to the next. It's outside of our control, forcing us to reconsider
everything we thought about life and relationships.

But being exposed is a good thing. By ourselves we can make
only the changes in our lives we're comfortable with. We get to hold
on to some of the comfortable things that have defined us. Marriage,
at its best, however, is where we can be exposed, but without fear
of judgment and condemnation. In a godly marriage, we are moving toward full exposure with maximum grace from each other and
from the Lord.

As we do, our live shots expose context and character, filling
our lives with so much more goodness than a snapshot could ever
express.

The live shot in all its glory is a picture of what the Bible refers
to as sanctification.

Sanctification is the term that describes how God takes us from
where we are to where He wants us to be. In the case of marriage,
that place is from *me* to *we*—oneness.

As we enter marriage, as we seek the Lord, we begin to grow individually with God and together in God. Our *me* becomes *we* as we
begin the process of fulfilling God's purposes for our lives, starting
with oneness.

Our marriage—our live shot—is the beginning of a process of growth and sanctification that God allows each of us to share in helping to cultivate the other.

Ephesians 5:26-33 shows how God allows us to share in cultivating each other in marriage:

> Husbands, love your wives, as Christ loved the church and gave himself up for her, that he might sanctify her, having cleansed her by the washing of water with the word, so that he might present the church to himself in splendor, without spot or wrinkle or any such thing, that she might be holy and without blemish. In the same way husbands should love their wives as their own bodies. He who loves his wife loves himself. For no one ever hated his own flesh, but nourishes and cherishes it, just as Christ does the church, because we are members of his body. "Therefore a man shall leave his father and mother and hold fast to his wife, and the two shall become one flesh." This mystery is profound, and I am saying that it refers to Christ and the church. However, let each one of you love his wife as himself, and let the wife see that she respects her husband.

These words aren't the whole of God's call on us in our spousal relationships, but here we find amazing imagery and purpose.

Paul, in speaking to men, tells them to love their wives as Christ loved the church. He's encouraging men to care for their wives as much as God loved each of us in coming to earth, giving up Himself and dying. He shares that in so doing, God was washing us. He was cleansing us and purifying us. The comparison between what God is doing in our lives individually and how it relates to our jobs in marriage can only be compared in terms of a mind-set. That's why Paul says he is referring to "Christ and the church," because there really is no comparison between Christ's role and ours.

This is beautiful imagery, but we promise you, the charge God is giving men within these passages is not found in a snapshot. It's found in the daily grind of serving selflessly. It's found in the live shot of giving without expecting anything in return. It's found in laying aside our own wants and needs.

Your Turn

What story do your pictures tell? What about your live shots reflects God's greatness in your life? What areas of your life do your live shots expose? Where do you need to grow most for your marriage to flourish?

Prayer

God, You are taking our marriage somewhere beautiful, but if I'm honest, I have to admit that sometimes I don't trust this truth. In the back of my mind I'm always a bit nervous and anxious as I feel myself losing control. Help me know and sense Your very real presence. Help me feel secure in You. You are my well-found confidence. As You expose me fully, may I be grace to my spouse and find their grace for me. May Your grace for each of us be the greatest, as You grow us individually and together. May I be able to say, "Clearly God is in this," and know that You are with me. In Jesus's name, amen.

5

Full of It

Jonathan

Wynter and I are nothing alike. She figured this out early in our relationship. I realized this was the case, too, but I tended to live in denial about it, and deep down I remained confident in my ability to change her—to shape and mold her, and to fill her with more of what I thought she needed: Me! Not Richard Gere!

Let's roll the tape back to an early and embarrassingly memorable conversation. I remember it as vividly as if it happened yesterday. I couldn't forget it, even if I wanted to.

We were sitting on the stoop of Wynter's apartment just a few minutes' walk from our college campus. The air was crisp, and our conversation was light. It was the kind of day I really enjoyed in Philadelphia in the early fall. We were discussing our future, as we did a lot during that year we were engaged. I had proposed to Wynter only eight months after meeting her, and though I never thought I would marry so young, I saw a bright future for us together, and I was optimistic about where our relationship would lead.

There was only one slight problem: my mind.

Somewhere in the conversation we began discussing what really mattered to us. You know, the deep things we would want to agree on when going into a lifelong commitment. I don't remember everything we discussed, but I wanted to come to some sort of pact about one topic, just to make sure we were on the same page.

Some people talk about the number of children they'd like to have or their preferred gender of said children. Others talk about where they would like to live or proximity to their in-laws. Wynter and I would have these conversations, but on this day, I fixated on something much more important to me at the time: fitness.

Over the years I had developed a love for fitness and exercise. Between sports, Boy Scouts, and Army ROTC, I had learned to discipline my body for both good health and self-esteem. I worked out on an almost daily basis, and without question physical fitness was a core value in my life.

Well, in our conversation, I decided to bring up this core value. It wasn't the first time I'd brought it up, because I had determined Wynter didn't hold this value in as high esteem as I did. I worked out daily and loved each session, but Wynter hadn't developed the same love. I decided her love for relaxation and rest instead equaled a lack of understanding and appreciation for her soon-to-be husband. As much as I tried to convince her to go to the gym with me and to help her understand this core value that was of most importance, she didn't seem to waver. But I was adamant about my superiority in this area, and I was convinced that I needed to drive my point home to win her over to my side.

In this vein of thinking, I made an ultimatum of sorts. To be fair to myself, I didn't understand the weight and gravity what I was about to say would carry. I only knew what I wanted, and it was important enough to me to take some risk.

And that's when I said it. It's almost impossible to write out as I think about it now.

"If you get fat, it will be hard for me to love you."

I should stop here to admit the insanity of my thought process. First, my wife weighed less than 110 pounds when I spoke those words. She also had and continues to have a gorgeous body that only God could design!

Feel free to hate me—at least to the end of this chapter. In my mind, I used these words only to help Wynter understand how much I valued health and fitness. At least that's what I was saying to myself. But in reality, I exposed a pretty ugly root in my own heart.

Luke 6:44-46 says,

> For each tree is known by its own fruit. Figs aren't gathered from thornbushes, or grapes picked from a bramble bush. A good person produces good out of the good stored up in his heart. An evil person produces evil out of the evil stored up in his heart, for his mouth speaks from the overflow of the heart (CSB).

It was my mouth overflowing, but it was my heart speaking. My heart was filled with vile poison, the perfect concoction of vanity and selfishness.

I wish I could say I repented in that moment and turned a new leaf. I wish I could tell you it was a moment of growth for me and that I understood the error of my ways. I wish I could say with confidence that I pulled that evil tree up by its roots and tossed it onto the street to wither and die.

Unfortunately, I cannot. I did not.

Yes, I did apologize and I did have remorse. It was not my goal to hurt. But I released a poison that not only ruined the moment, but put a stain on our engagement. Even more, it became a dagger in the side of my wife, and I would twist it when necessary to attempt to control and manipulate.

This story would drag on for years in our marriage. Those words quite simply exposed bitterness and evil that both Wynter and I were aware of. It created a noticeable distrust and insecurity in Wynter. It also left me miserable when I thought Wynter wasn't living up to my unrealistic expectations and wishes.

That thought and mind-set and all their poison needed to die. I'm sure some of you are thinking literally right now, but I needed to die at least figuratively.

I had "stored up" an evil mind-set that surely needed to be emptied.

Wynter

I am not a fan of personality tests. I have a few reasons for that, but the time it takes to complete them is probably the greatest reason. I'm guessing this might tell you a lot about my personality. On the other hand, Jonathan loves personality tests. As a matter of fact, he loves them so much that he'll often take mine for me, which I think says a lot about his personality! Maybe that's why we get along so well; He gets to do all the work and I reap the benefit.

If you're a personality test guru, then I'm sure the above paragraph has given you plenty of information to determine which letters or numbers reflect who I am, depending on the test of your choice. I'm guessing your guess is pretty accurate!

I may not like to take assessments, but I do trust the results and appreciate the insight.

The truth is I prefer someone else taking the test for me because it's just easier that way. And unfortunately, I've been known to choose the easier route many times throughout my life.

I can't deny that I like to take it easy. One of my absolute favorite things to do is sit quietly, alone, under a cozy blanket—lights optional. This sounds terrible to Jonathan, but I see it as a lovely time!

My testing quirks also accurately describe how I've tried to organize my life. I tend to not want to overcomplicate things, and I'll even resort to just giving up to make sure life stays simple.

This is not something I'm proud of, but it's true nonetheless. One of the deciding factors that led me to the university where I met Jonathan and received my undergraduate degree was that they offered an easy application process, and they didn't require an essay! It was just too simple to pass up! How ironic is it that I now love to write? At the time, however, I couldn't wrap my head around writing an essay when there was an option not to. I shied away from, totally avoided, and hid from anything that seemed to present too much of a challenge.

Another example is that, when I was a senior in high school and just a few months shy of graduation, I decided I was no longer going to complete projects. That's right, I decided that regardless of the days remaining on the calendar, I was done. I was already accepted into the college of my choice, my grades were good, and my senior photos had been taken. Quite frankly, I was tired of working and didn't see the point. When I respectfully announced to my history teacher that I would not be turning in my last project, he informed me that the zero would affect my grade. Two steps ahead of him, I fully expected that, and I was prepared to deal with the consequence.

As I said, overall my grades were good, so one zero wouldn't make a huge impact.

When I made this same announcement to my African-American Literature teacher, however, he informed me he would use the incomplete as a reason to fail me, meaning he would give me a zero for his entire class and prohibit me from walking across the stage in my upcoming graduation. I remember being so frustrated with him! I could not fathom why he was being so mean to me! In my mind, this last project didn't matter. I had already worked enough to make it to the next step in my academic journey, so what was the point?

My African-American Literature teacher observed something in me that you probably saw in me as soon as you started reading this section. I don't mind working, but my natural tendency is to do only what is required of me and nothing more. The second some task becomes a little too time consuming, demands too much of me, or forces me out of my comfort zone, I look for an easy way out. He was determined not to let me, and years later, I thanked him for it.

I don't know where this started. I'm not sure if it's a learned behavior based on my environment or if it's rooted in my innate sin nature. It's most likely a combination of both. My mother never pushed me too hard; she preferred to see me happy over working. I don't blame her. I do know if I'm not careful, though, the lasting results this type of laziness breeds can be devastating.

Because you're reading this book, I assume you know the institution of marriage, in and of itself, is not easy, and that when viewed as a covenant ordained by God, there is no easy route. Becoming one with Jonathan has forced me out of every comfort zone I've ever tried to settle into, has consumed more time than I've ever thought available, and has demanded all of me, daily.

Now, don't get me wrong. I have tried to get out. One day within the first year of our marriage, Jonathan and I had a huge fight in our two-bedroom apartment, with yelling, screaming, and door slamming. The scene resembled that of two strong-willed, spoiled, and uncontrollable toddlers—but in this case, with 23-year-olds. After several minutes of this, I decided I'd had enough. I made my announcement, similar to the one I'd made to my literature teacher in high school. I was done doing the work, and I was okay with the consequence. After letting Jonathan know it was over, I turned around, stormed out of the apartment, and slammed the door behind me.

Have you ever been there? When things just seemed too overwhelming to salvage, and leaving, either physically, emotionally, or mentally, seemed like the best, if not the only, option? For me, what we were building together no longer seemed worth the hard work required of me. It was still early enough for me to count my losses and move on to an easier way of life.

After about two hours, I came back. Well, Jonathan brought me back. When I stormed out, I forgot one minor detail: I had nowhere to go. After getting lost in our neighborhood, I called him for directions to get back home. Once we both had some time to calm down, Jonathan looked at me and said, "Babe, leaving is not an option. Remove those words from your vocabulary." Those words zapped my emotions into place and took up permanent residence in my heart.

Jonathan saw something I had not. I saw emotion and hard work. I saw a test I was not necessarily willing to take. I was ready to run. He saw purpose beyond the emotion, and he was ready to fight. Regardless of who was wrong or right in this instance, I learned that night that my marriage was not about my comfort. Failing to finish this God-ordained assignment was not an option.

My desire to throw in the towel has always been about my comfort. It has always been about finding what is easy and convenient. Marriage was a new test for me. I brought my same old habits into it, but thankfully, Jonathan saw something completely different, and so did God. In my loss of comfort, God began to deal with my desire for false comforts in exchange for the real thing. It was also the very place and testing God used to convict, correct, and show me the value of hope, follow-through, and the benefit in the struggle.

This Scripture about bad and good fruit has such good imagery for us as we consider the fruit we bring into our marriages. Let's look at it again.

> For each tree is known by its own fruit. Figs aren't gathered from thornbushes, or grapes picked from a bramble bush. A good person produces good out of the good stored up in his heart. An evil person produces evil out of the evil stored up in his heart, for his mouth speaks from the overflow of the heart (Luke 6:44-46 CSB).

Certainly we brought good fruit into our marriage. We were both committed to being faithful followers of Jesus Christ, albeit immature. We both wanted to honor the Lord. We both felt like God was calling us to a life of purpose together. We both had an image in our minds that was holy and good.

But we also brought bad fruits that were poisonous to the fullness of what God would have for our marriage and future. The more time we spent together, the more we knew it. The more time we spent with God, the more we were convicted by it. The pruning process would include forgiveness of sin, even sin we each committed prior to entering marriage. We would have to deal with our history. Moving forward wouldn't be possible without digging into some things that had built up over time. And it would most certainly include the breaking down of expectations we had placed on each other that weren't godly or even reasonable.

The pruning process would be a pruning of the heart.

The imagery given to us in John 15:1-8 was what was needed in our marriage, and we're certain is needed in yours as well.

> I am the true vine, and my Father is the vinedresser. Every branch in me that does not bear fruit he takes away, and every branch that does bear fruit he prunes, that it may bear more fruit. Already you are clean because of the word that I have spoken to you. Abide in me, and I in you. As the branch cannot bear fruit by itself, unless it abides in the vine, neither can you, unless you abide in me. I am the vine; you are the branches. Whoever abides in me and I in him, he it is that bears much fruit, for apart from me you can do nothing. If anyone does not abide in me he is thrown away like a branch and withers; and the branches are gathered, thrown into the fire, and burned. If you abide in me, and my words abide in you, ask whatever you wish, and it will be done for you. By this my Father is glorified, that you bear much fruit and so prove to be my disciples.

We thank God that we belong to Him—to the vineyard keeper. We are grateful to be attached to the vine—Jesus Christ. He spoke to us at very young ages and began to trim us and shape us for His

purposes. He introduced us. The Lord has used our marriage and
relationship to continue to prune us and shape us to bear more fruit
in and through our marriage. We needed—and continue to need—
to be pruned of all the sin, history, and expectations that so easily
hold us up. God has been and continues to be faithful to do this,
always taking us back to His purpose for bringing us together in the
first place. He had a standard in mind for us, and He has the same
standard in mind for you, working toward it one pruned branch at
a time.

We needed to be emptied of a whole bunch of bad fruit. These
stories were just early signs.

So many of us go into marriage thinking we have what it takes
to build what God has in mind for our marriages. We go in with
arrogant attitudes and puffed-up spirits. We are filled with pride
and brimming with confidence. If we're really feeling ourselves, we
believe we have everything it takes to make it on our own and to fill
our spouse's tanks.

Jonathan

> Early and often God reminded me how
> little I had to offer Wynter and how much
> I needed from Him myself.

I was about as prideful as anyone could be. Not only did I feel like
I was bringing fantastic good fruit to our marriage, but I was certain
that my very presence would be enough to fill Wynter with what I
thought she needed. Having dated her, and then been engaged to
her for over a year, I knew some of the wounds Wynter had, and I
thought I was just the man to deal with them. I thought to myself,

It won't take me long to whip her into shape. I laugh at that now! How naïve I was. But early and often God reminded me how little I had to offer Wynter and how much I needed from Him myself.

I found myself broken, over and over, realizing that what I was bringing to the table wasn't enough. My efforts, my skill, my will power, and my hard work were not enough.

In this place, I realized this was exactly where God wanted me. Broken. Surrendered. And ready to pour out my efforts, my skill, my willpower, and my hard work in an act of symbolically waving the white flag.

You see, I knew theoretically how this worked. Remember, I was a follower of Jesus. I knew what Scripture has to say about what we offer in this life. The entirety of the gospel is about surrender. It's about giving up, though not in the way Wynter tried with her teachers.

Wynter

It wasn't that I was prideful in an *I'll fix Jonathan* kind of way. It was quite the opposite. I came into marriage thinking we would be just fine. I tend to approach life that way. Just show up, have a little faith, and everything will fall into place. I assumed Jonathan would handle his business, and I would ignore mine. I wasn't interested in dealing with any "wounds," as Jonathan would describe them, and I certainly didn't expect to deal with his!

> I needed to confront the areas of my life that required change. I could no longer sweep my brokenness under a rug while believing God for healing.

I knew God's Word, and I was committed to learning more. I

read books, memorized Bible verses, and waited patiently for any necessary changes to occur. Now that I was doing life God's way, He would make everything fall into place. But I was missing one major piece: Knowing God's Word was just the beginning. Living it out was an altogether different story. I needed to confront the areas of my life that required change. I could no longer sweep my brokenness under a rug while believing God for healing. For Christ to heal, I needed to show up with my wounds exposed and surrender my comfort.

Paul reminds us of the commitment we need to have in Galatians 2:20. A commitment to giving up. A commitment to being emptied.

> I have been crucified with Christ; and it is no longer I who live, but Christ lives in me; and the life which I now live in the flesh I live by faith in the Son of God, who loved me and gave Himself up for me (NASB).

In this Scripture, Paul was speaking directly to his Christian brothers and sisters who were allowing race and tradition to separate them, including the apostle Peter. Their preferences, concerns, and fears were causing relational conflict, which was antithetical to the gospel. He rebuked them in their thinking that they could maintain control of what they'd brought into their Christian faith—sin, history, and tradition—and reminded them of who they were in Christ. He reminded them of how they were supposed to live as Christ followers.

He reminded them that when they decided to follow Jesus, and when Jesus pulled them out of their life of hopelessness in exchange for lives full of His grace, they died. He told them their lives were now lives of full submission to Jesus, and that it was Him, in them, directing and controlling their lives. He would go on to remind them that only through God's grace would they live full, good lives!

Ultimately, Paul was telling these early followers of Jesus and us today that to win, we must be willing to lose. We must be willing to lose our lives—our flesh, our control—to allow Jesus to fully express Himself and live His life inside us.

Just as for Peter and his friends, it took conflict for us to realize we were each working tirelessly to hold on to control and comfort. And just as it was for Peter, God called us to a place of surrender in a place of confrontation.

This Scripture should give each of us hope as we consider two things. First, if the people Paul was talking to were all first- and second-generation Christians, those who lived while Jesus walked the earth and others just one generation past, yet they could forget who they were in Jesus, how much more are we prone to forget? Second, God isn't asking us to try harder in our Christian lives; He's asking us to commit to letting go, to surrendering.

Your Turn

Bad fruit comes into our marriages in different ways, such as pride, vanity, slothfulness, and selfishness. In most cases these fruits exist out of our desire to control and manipulate, and our tendency to project. What bad fruits have you brought into marriage? How ready are you to die to these fruits to pursue the life and marriage God wants for you?

Prayer

Father, You speak very clearly of the harm rotten fruit
has in my life, and you're just as clear about Your desire
to see it pruned away completely. May I not be content to allow the rotten fruit in my life to poison my
marriage. Rather, may I willingly surrender and submit
to Your process of pruning. May I trust that You don't
break me to destroy me, but that You break me to grow
me. Help me to see this process as an investment in my
Christlike character that will pay dividends for generations to come and eternally. In Jesus's name, amen.

6

Mind-Set

Being emptied in marriage is a mind-set. It's a way of life. It's less about our ability to try harder, not at all about our ability to grind it out. It's more about our ability to have an altogether different mind than what we believe we want in our natural state of being. It's altogether different from the mind-set constantly advertised to us in this world. A simple Scripture describes it best:

> Do not conform to the pattern of this world, but be transformed by the renewing of your mind. Then you will be able to test and approve what God's will is—his good, pleasing and perfect will (Romans 12:2 NIV).

Our emptiness is the only state where we will be renewed and transformed.

In our lives and in our marriages, God is offering us the opportunity to be transformed. He is inviting us on a journey of having our minds renewed. But our emptiness is the only state where we will be renewed and transformed. Being filled with "the pattern of this world" stands in contrast to being transformed and renewed in our minds. We must come to a place of surrendering those patterns and being emptied of them to be filled with the very things that will bring about God's will, which He describes as good, pleasing, and perfect!

Do you want your marriage to be good, pleasing, and perfect? Then ask the Lord to begin working on your mind. Ask Him to remove those patterns and thoughts that exist today in exchange for His patterns and thoughts.

Let's talk a little bit about God's mind-set, and then more specifically about Jesus's mind-set as He made the decision to follow God's will for our sake and for our relationship with Him.

To begin, we need to understand that God's mind-set was all about the restoration of perfection. He knew that to arrive at perfection, a restoration would need to occur. Because we are made in God's image and handcrafted by a master architect and builder, each one of us look well maintained on the outside. From a distance, it's easy to be impressed and wowed, but the closer we get to one another, the easier it is to pull out the other's flaws, blemishes, and stains.

Proximity makes all the difference in the world.

We're not saying this is a wrong thing, but we are saying it's a thing. Because we're made in the image of God, we all have a desire to be around beauty. We like new. We like shiny. We like our bathrooms to be clean. We like our cars to smell fresh and the carpet to be vacuumed. We prefer our hair groomed and our socks crisp.

And regardless of your theology or your culture, you can find this reality somewhere in your personality.

Well, there's nothing wrong with aspiring for perfection. We're hardwired that way. You just need to know that you'll never arrive there, and we need to have the same mind-set our spouses have. God is the master craftsman who perfectly designed you and your spouse. Blemishes will arise, and imperfections will appear, but God wants to move you toward His perfect will. Remember, God's will for you is good, pleasing, and perfect. Another word used to describe that is *holy*.

In Leviticus 11:44 God says, "I am the LORD your God. Consecrate yourselves therefore, and be holy, for I am holy."

Holiness. To some it's an old-school Christian term, but God does call us to holiness. Holiness can be described a few ways. It includes the sense of being clean or set apart. It speaks of God's otherness and His transcendence. It implies His sinlessness and purity. In God's holiness we gaze in astonishment and wonder and get to see a glimpse of His magnificence.

> **God's will is for our lives and marriages to be holy, set apart, altogether different**

God's will is for our lives and marriages to be holy, set apart, altogether different from those lives and marriages following the patterns of the world. The world will say marriage is no big deal, and that the commitment in marriage is optional and flexible. Couples that understand what it means to be renewed in their mind by God's Spirit, however, will say marriage is a big deal, and that their perspectives on their relationships matter now and for eternity. The world would have them say, *My emotions and my desires are more important than my spouse's.* In marriages renewed by God's Spirit and following after Him, the spouses would each say, *It's my job to serve my spouse, and I should be willing to lay down my emotions and my desires, if necessary, to value my spouse.*

Marriages renewed by God's Spirit and seeking His will are beautiful. If we take this mind-set into our marriages, we will experience beauty and will be putting God's beauty on display for others around us.

Each one of us appreciates this type of marriage and relationship. We cry when we see it on television or in the movies. We're motivated by it when we see another couple in church or in our neighborhood that walk this walk. We love to see this level of commitment when we're strolling through the mall—you know, that senior couple walking, not even shopping, the gentleman's bride holding his arm like she has since they were married decades ago.

It's fun to see, but it's also what God has for us and for you. We know this innately because He has placed this desire in our consciousness. We long for His standard, and God calls each of us to that standard. He tells us throughout the Bible to "be holy, for I am holy," as in 1 Peter 1:16.

Sounds simple right? God calls us to this standard in every area of our lives, and He certainly calls us to this standard in our marriages. He expects perfection, and He will accept nothing short of it. Hebrews 11:4 alludes to this very fact: "Let marriage be held in honor among all, and let the marriage bed be undefiled, for God will judge the sexually immoral and adulterous."

We have some good news! Some of it will sound good now, and some of it will sound good later.

The good news is you are not left alone to clean yourself up. And you aren't left alone to purify your marriage. God desires to join you in bringing about His will. We don't know about you, but that allows us to breathe a huge sigh of relief.

God alone is the creator of your beauty, and He is the maintainer. He built the house, and He will maintain the house. He assumes the responsibility. He has gone through all the hard work to completely restore the beauty and magnificence of your life and marriage.

He tells us to simply look to Him: "[Look] to Jesus, the founder and perfecter of our faith, who for the joy that was set before him endured the cross, despising the shame, and is seated at the right hand of the throne of God" (Hebrews 12:2).

The key is looking to Him. For His restoration and cleaning process to begin, all you need to do is acknowledge Him as the builder and welcome Him in as the restorer. I love how the book of Revelation says it, when we're told Jesus says to us, "Here I am! I stand at the door and knock. If anyone hears my voice and opens the door, I will come in and eat with that person, and they with me" (3:20 NIV).

God isn't interested in just cleaning you up; He wants to be in a relationship with you as well. It's not a once-and-done job. He wants to be a part of your life, your home, your marriage.

That's good news!

Here's the news that might not sound as good at first glance, especially if you picked up this book because you were more interested in cleaning up or fixing your spouse.

God wants you to be more interested in His dealing with you than in His dealing with your spouse.

God wants you to be more interested in His dealing with you than in His dealing with your spouse. He basically says, "Let Me deal with them while I deal with you. Let Me grow with them while I grow with you."

Now, God does invite you into the process. He doesn't say, "Stay out of this!" But the part of the process He invites you into is the part that most of us would rather not take head-on.

He invites each of us to imitate Him, but also to "die."

This might not seem appealing to your ears, but we promise you it should. Hang in there with us. To experience the fullness God has for your relationship, you must begin the process of a poured-out marriage. This imagery might be a bit difficult to understand, but we see it in the life of Jesus. We see it in exploring what Jesus did for you and for us—His bride, as He calls us, the bride of Christ.

In our relationships with our spouses, Jesus asks us to join Him on a road most of us wouldn't volunteer for. Yet He doesn't ask us to do anything He hasn't already done.

Jesus, our author and perfecter, went down a road of brutality, torture, death, and separation from God that you and we will never have to experience. His death paid for our sins and allowed us the opportunity to have relationship with Him. And He calls us to think like He thinks, so we can act like He acts.

But He hasn't left us alone. He has given us His mind. In 1 Corinthians 2:16, Paul encourages his readers (and us!) by writing, "We have the mind of Christ." Jesus tells us to follow Him, but He also tells us we have His mind—if we are His followers. He tells us to give up our lives. He says that in so doing, we are saving our lives:

> If anyone wishes to come after Me, he must deny himself, and take up his cross daily and follow Me. For whoever wishes to save his life will lose it, but whoever loses his life for My sake, he is the one who will save it (Luke 9:23-24 NASB).

He asks us to carry ourselves with the same mind-set with which He carried Himself.

We need to ask ourselves a few questions. What was Jesus's mind-set? What was He thinking when He laid down His life for us? How did His thinking affect His action?

> God has a specific vision for our marriage and yours,
> a standard higher than anything we will ever
> reach on our own.

God has a specific vision for our marriage and yours, a standard higher than anything we will ever reach on our own. His standard is perfection. His request is that we be holy—set apart, magnificent, and otherworldly. He doesn't want you to have a common marriage. Thankfully, He has not left you alone to try to reach this standard. He has stepped down into your life and into your marriage, and He offers you the help you need. But He wants to start with you, individually. He will get to your spouse, but He is asking you to invite Him in, to allow Him to clean you up. He wants to expose the stains. He wants to make your marriage fruitful. And He starts by offering you more of His mind, more of Himself. He created you. He arranged your marriage. He will perfect it, starting in your mind.

Your Turn

We've talked a lot about ourselves. We've shared quite a bit about the expectations, sin, and history we brought into our marriage. We imagine you might feel encouraged by some parts of what you've read, slightly discouraged by others, and overwhelmed by it all.

Remember, there is good news, starting with the fact that God goes into the ring with you. It's His fight. You only need to look to Him and choose to allow Him to fight for you.

Let's take some time and do that, starting with answering some questions requiring transparency:

1. To this point, what has defined your vision of marriage and driven your expectations? How does that compare to God's vision for your marriage?
2. We shared some specific attitudes we brought into our marriage that were easy to see needed to be emptied out. What sin/habit/attitude do you want to ask the Lord to empty from your life?
3. We talked about our live shot and the reality that our relationship is filled with imperfection that has given context and color we've come to appreciate to our story. What parts of your story and live shot do you need to begin embracing, asking God to show you their beauty?
4. What sin/habit/attitude does your spouse currently have that you are deciding to give to God in prayer as opposed to trying to hold on to it?

As we move into the next part of the book, we pray that the Lord will open your eyes and your heart, and that He will begin to renew your mind and your marriage, moving you toward His good, pleasing, and perfect will.

Prayer

Heavenly Father, thank You for the life You have given me. Thank You for [spouse's name]. Thank You for bringing us from where we were, baggage and all, and bringing us together to form a *we* out of a *me*. As we begin to embrace our live shot and continue our journey of growing in You, individually and together, may Your grace and mercy be ever present. May I choose to focus my heart and mind on You, Jesus, leaving [spouse's name] for You to work on.

May You begin to show me the areas of my life that need to be poured out. May You begin to grant me the power to do the pouring. May Your mind become mine, and may I grow in my understanding and experience of Christlikeness toward my spouse. May I be emptied so that You can begin to fill me up with more of You. In Jesus's name, amen.

7

Emptied

Wynter

I can think of one specific attitude Jonathan brought into marriage that has been a real benefit to me and our family. He is a willing helper any day of the week. God has given him an amazing work ethic and a willingness to sacrifice whatever is necessary to provide and bring convenience.

I never have to think about picking up a prescription for one of our kids in the middle of the night. And I can count on my fingers the number of times I've had to go grocery shopping this year; in every case, Jonathan was out of town. My man can go!

He hasn't always done the grocery shopping, but right after I delivered our twins, it was extremely difficult for me to leave the house. So Jonathan absorbed the responsibility with no complaints. Now our youngest girls are well beyond keeping me from leaving the house, but Jonathan continues to shop, visiting three or four stores to bring home all the essentials five girls need to survive!

I used to take this for granted, but I now realize the level of commitment he has to me and to us. Even in this small illustration, I'm proud to say that Jonathan's willingness to serve me has been one small win on our way from *me* to *we*.

Jonathan

Soon after we married, it was rather difficult for me to see some of the attitudes Wynter brought to our marriage that were a benefit. It's taken me a while to appreciate them, but now they are like a life-line. Let's start with patience and calm. Her ability to relax despite the pressure of everything going on around her is amazing. Honestly, it's probably what first drew me to her, even though I didn't realize it at the time.

I always operate with a bit of anxiety in my soul. It's hard for me to sit still and rest unless I'm really worn down, but Wynter has always been a calming force. She's easygoing and able to calm my soul even when I'd prefer to freak out. Take for example the writing we get to do together. I experience the deadline internally, even several months before the project is due. Or take our girls. She can slowly breathe in all that's happening with our four daughters, removing the intensity and filtering all the excitement that over-whelms me on many days.

Calling out your spouse's beneficial attributes
is a sure way to remain grateful for the person
God has placed in your life.

We mention these attributes because it's important to recognize Christlikeness in each other on a routine basis. Calling out your spouse's beneficial attributes is a sure way to remain grateful for the person God has placed in your life. Remember, we are all made in God's image, so calling out those characteristics has a way of making you feel better about your spouse and grateful to God for the gifts He has given you in them. It's also a simple way to make sure they feel appreciated for who they are.

Each of us has some Christlike attitudes we operate with on a normal basis, but we also have a ton of room to grow. We won't grow on our own, but we also can't grow in an area we don't understand.

Knowing where our attitudes, good and bad, come from will have a direct result on our ability to move forward.

Jonathan

Remember that embarrassing story I told you about when I said I wouldn't be able to love Wynter if she gained weight? That story comes from an old attitude stored deep down inside. It would need to be uprooted, but it would first need to be understood.

I was in the ninth grade and brand-new to my high school. Having grown up as one of only a few mixed-race kids in my middle school, I never felt like I fit in. The only other two bi-racial people I remember being in my eighth grade class were my twin brother and cousin.

I was determined to fit in at high school. I didn't want to do anything that would make me stand out, at least not negatively. So I would try to dress like most of the kids in my school—you know, be as normal as possible. And I would try to act like most of the kids. The jocks seemed like a good group of guys to join, so I started there. My attitude was one of assimilation. In my mind, I figured that had to be better than being so different. I never felt like I fit in with the white kids, and I never felt like I fit in with the black kids.

Just a few months into my freshman year, I took note of a teacher I admired. He carried himself well. He looked sharp. He was well respected in our community, and everything about him screamed success.

One day, as I was walking by his classroom around lunchtime, I saw his wife go in there. She had their infant with her, and she was dressed down. To me she seemed a bit unkempt. Their baby was just a few weeks old, so she was also still carrying a bit of her baby weight.

A negative attitude entered my 14-year-old mind as a few thoughts rushed into my head. What's mind-boggling about this memory is that it all happened in a few split seconds. I was literally just walking by, and I didn't enter the room. I didn't even stop. But in ten seconds, I opened a door for the Enemy to plant a seed that would affect my marriage for many years.

I thought to myself, *Why would she do that to him? Why wouldn't she take better care of herself? I will never marry a girl who doesn't take better care of herself.*

I still can't believe this memory is so vivid in my mind. It's stuck with me all these years, and it's the earliest realization of resentment in this area. In the book of Deuteronomy, God speaks of this type of resentment when He says,

> Beware lest there be among you a man or woman or clan or tribe whose heart is turning away today from the LORD our God to go and serve the gods of those nations. Beware lest there be among you a root bearing poisonous and bitter fruit (Deuteronomy 29:18).

In harboring those thoughts, I solidified a mind-set and an

attitude that was unhealthy and would ultimately become idola-
try. My attitude became so fixed and so deep that it became another
god altogether.

An idol, simply put, is anything you put before God and anything you serve and worship over God. My idol wasn't even a real
thing. It was an idea. It was a notion of a future I wanted so badly
that it caused me to tell my fiancée my love for her would be con-
tingent upon her weight.

Thankfully, God knew each of us would bring these sorts of idols
and images into our lives and into our marriages.

Let's explore what Jesus was thinking about and the attributes
He brought to this earth that are examples for us to follow.

These attributes led Him to a place that granted our freedom,
hope, and eternal life. His mind-set gave us the most intimate relationship we will ever have, and those gifts can bring real intimacy
into our marriages, should we walk in them.

The more you come to understand His heart for you, the more
you'll fall in love with Him. The more you can comprehend His
mind-set, the more you'll realize the depths He was willing to go to
reveal His love.

So what was Jesus's mind-set?

We can't think of a better place to go than to the book of Philippians. Paul, speaking to the Christians in Philippi, tells us exactly
what Jesus's mind-set was when He died for us:

> Have this attitude in yourselves which was also in Christ
> Jesus, who, although He existed in the form of God, did
> not regard equality with God a thing to be grasped, but
> emptied Himself, taking the form of a bond-servant,
> and being made in the likeness of men. Being found in
> appearance as a man, He humbled Himself by becom-
> ing obedient to the point of death, even death on a cross
> (Philippians 2:5-8 NASB).

"Have this attitude," Paul begins. *Attitude.* That's a funny word to use.

Attitudes, as we know them, come in two specific varieties. Pos-itive or negative. Fruitful or unfruitful. Productive or unproductive. Most certainly, we all bring both varieties into marriage, and we're willing to bet you agree that, one way or another, our attitudes have drastic consequences built in.

The King James Version of the Bible says it so well in verse 5: "Let this mind be in you."

It's sort of an impossible thought, right? We have human minds, and those minds shape our attitudes. That's what we love about Scripture and about God's specific word to us. He encourages us to do something both He and we know we can't do on our own. He says we aren't there yet, and that's why He encourages us. Conversely, He tells us we have that very thing.

For example, in one Scripture He tells us we "have the mind of Christ" (1 Corinthians 2:16 NASB). Yet in another place He says, "Have this attitude in yourselves which was also in Christ Jesus" (Philippians 2:5 NASB).

The first implies we already have God's mind. The next encour-ages us to have His mind! Theologians refer to this as the "already but not yet." You and I live in a world where God is calling us something we are not—holy. And He is calling us to do something we can't do—be holy. Nevertheless, Christlikeness is our call and our position. Have this attitude in yourselves—encouragement. You have the mind of Christ—affirmation.

Whatever the idols and whatever the images, God wants to replace them. In one sense He already has; in another, He is still displacing them in our lives—if we are followers of Jesus.

He is removing specific mind-sets, and He is replacing them with others.

Philippians 2:7 says Jesus "emptied himself." What a phrase and what a mind-set. This is an attitude we can all learn from!

We are full of sin, history, expectations, and a whole myriad of things that are ungodly, but Jesus was full of something altogether different. Verse 6 tells us that "[Jesus,] who, although He existed in the form of God, did not regard equality with God a thing to be grasped" (NASB).

Jesus was full of deity. Speaking in human terms, He was God when He decided to come to earth to save us from our sins. He had every reason to reconsider His attitude and mind-set that would save us. Nevertheless, He moved forward. He emptied Himself of every reason and everything that would stop Him from completing His mission. He emptied Himself of anything that would stop Him from bearing our sins. He made Himself nothing by taking the very nature of a servant and humbling Himself.

His mind-set was not one of pride or entitlement.

What would it look like for us to empty ourselves of anything and everything that keeps us from accomplishing the mission of God in our marriages?

What would it look like for us to take on this attitude? What would it look like for us to empty ourselves of anything and everything that keeps us from accomplishing the mission of God in our marriages? Jesus laid aside the perfection of heaven to serve humanity. How much more should we empty ourselves of things that are far less holy, and in many cases sinful or evil, to serve like He served?

Taking on the mind of Christ can seem a bit daunting and difficult to understand, but let's look at four practical themes that describe His mind-set.

Likeness of Men

With an attitude of emptiness, Jesus decided to become a man. This decision is easy to gloss over. *He's God, so what's the big deal?* we might think.

It's almost like thinking about Superman coming from Krypton to serve humans. He decides to limit his powers as Clark Kent and dress and live like ordinary Metropolis citizens. He works a normal job at *The Planet* and deals with the ups and downs, hurts and pains, and complications of the life we live.

Well, Jesus did do that. But He did more. The Bible says He went much further to be able to empathize with us in our weakness. Our High Priest is not one who cannot feel empathy for our weaknesses. On the contrary, He was tempted in every way we are, though He did not sin.

He was also tortured and mocked. He was brutally killed. He experienced the worst humanity had to give and the most Satan could dish out. He did it so we could experience an amazing relationship and oneness with Him.

What would it look like for us to take on this attitude? Jesus laid aside His equality with God. He came down from a pedestal of perfection to serve the least of us, and He asks us to come down from our imperfect pedestals to serve our imperfect partners. He is asking us to adopt a mind-set of lowliness. He is asking us to consider the needs of our imperfect partners, like He considered the needs of His imperfect people.

Humility

Jesus kept emptying Himself. Not many of us are willing to be subjected to insult without the option of hurling one back. Contrast that mind-set with that of our Lord and Savior. Jesus didn't even open His mouth!

The Old Testament prophet Isaiah spoke predictively of Jesus when he shared this prophecy: "He was oppressed, and he was afflicted, yet he opened not his mouth: he is brought as a lamb to the slaughter, and as a sheep before her shearers is dumb, so he openeth not his mouth" (Isaiah 53:7 KJV).

Though Jesus is accurately described as a lion throughout the Bible, strong and fierce, He emptied Himself to the point of lamb-like tendencies when He was taking on our distress. When He was carrying the burdens that should have been ours, He did not try to run. He did not look for a way of escape. He didn't even open His mouth. No cursing, no making excuses. No anger toward those who put Him there, and no vitriol toward His foes.

What would it look like for us to take on this attitude? What would it look like to listen to our spouses without grumbling, even when we disagree? To admit our fault even if we feel we've "won" the argument? To ask for forgiveness when our relationships are torn? What would it look like for us to willingly refrain from making excuses, yelling, fighting, and hurling insults? What if we willingly closed our mouths for the benefit of our significant other?

Obedience

Jesus became our bond-servant. He entered humanity, and He became the humblest man to ever walk the face of this earth. He did all this as the ultimate act of obedience. You see, He wasn't acting on His own; He was submitting to the will of the Father.

In speaking to the Father, Jesus would say, "Abba! Father! All things are possible for You; remove this cup from Me; yet not what I will, but what You will" (Mark 14:36 NASB).

Jesus, in His humanity as the God-Man, had no desire to go through what He was about to go through. Absolutely none. In the New Testament, we find Him asking the Father for permission to lay aside this responsibility. He begs God, asking if it's possible for Him to find another way. This wasn't a plan He hadn't fully considered; He'd thought through the difficulty. But while kneeling in prayer in the garden of Gethsemane, just a short walk from where He would suffer and die, Jesus asked the Father to change His mind.

What an eye-opener! In our humanity, we don't have to want the difficulties in our marriages, the tough situations we're going through, and our real suffering in this imperfect world. It's understandable that we don't want to suffer. It's acceptable that we not feel good about some of what we have to go through. We don't have to feel guilty about these thoughts. Nevertheless, it is the call.

Look at how Jesus handles these thoughts. He says, "Yet not what I will, but what You will" (Mark 14:36 NASB). He submits His will to the Father's will. He lays aside His desire for God's desire. He takes inventory, has a gut check, and proceeds to follow through with the impossible for us all.

What would it look like for us to take on this attitude? To take inventory of all that is difficult about our marriages or even all that is "wrong" with our spouses, and willingly lay aside our desires for the Father's? To make a well-measured decision to be obedient to the Lord? To stick it out? To endure? And to pursue renewed relationship, whatever the cost?

Called to Die

Philippians 2:8 says, "Being found in appearance as a man, He humbled Himself by becoming obedient to the point of death, even death on a cross" (NASB).

Death is a difficult topic most of us would prefer not to approach. With death comes separation from all that we know. It means walking into an unknown that seems bleak, meaningless, and void of hope.

But death is a reality Christ faced head-on, willingly and purposefully. He walked into it, knowing that with His death, life would come for us.

What would it look like for us to take on this attitude? To have a "whatever the cost" boldness that would cause us to move toward an existence we've never considered, a reality we didn't think possible? What if we made the decision to face a nonreality to bring about life for our spouses?

In 1 John 3:16 we read, "We know what real love is because Jesus gave up his life for us. So we also ought to give up our lives for our brothers and sisters" (NLT). Thankfully, most of us will not have to face literal death like Jesus did. The odds are in your favor that you will never have to carry out death in your physical body to save your spouse.

But each of us is called to a figurative death to further the story of God's kingdom purpose in our marriage. We are called to have this mind-set. That is what the next pages will detail, but they will also share the joy that can be found in the endeavor.

Considering what it looks like to live like Jesus lived is a
daunting task. Thankfully, we don't have to muster the
strength on our own nor carry the cost.

Considering what it looks like to live like Jesus lived is a daunt-ing task. Thankfully, we don't have to muster the strength on our own nor carry the cost; that is too big a burden. In the pages ahead, we'll discuss how we have found power much greater than ourselves that came alongside us to help in our weakness.

We're speaking of the Spirit of God—"the Helper" as He is referred to. You see, we have the power to face death—albeit figura-tively in most cases—only through the presence and power of God and through an authority and nature that is foreign to us before we receive it by faith.

We thank God that His power and His power alone has given us the strength to continue the journey of dying daily for each other. And it's in this power that we'll continue.

Your Turn

Think of one specific trait, attitude, and skill that your spouse has brought into your marriage that you typically take for granted. Write each down and then briefly describe in what ways each enhances your marriage. What is one trait, attitude, or action that you've brought into marriage that simply needs to be poured out and emptied?

Prayer

Heavenly Father, it's much easier to spot my spouse's flaws than my own. And it's much easier for me to see my strengths while focusing on my partner's weaknesses. Lord, help me to have a change in perspective that begins with altering my focus. Instead of an attitude of pride and self-righteousness, may I take on a disposition of humility and self-sacrifice. May I no longer look to be served, but may I serve. May Your Spirit's power give me the help and strength I need to walk like Christ. Though I will never know the experience of giving up perfection, I can know the experience of pouring out my life for someone else. May you begin to turn my heart, mind, and every action toward one of emptiness. In Jesus's name, amen.

8

Filled

God is our...very present help in trouble.

PSALM 46:1

Jonathan

My wife is an easygoing girl. She's a mellow personality, and by nature unassuming. I've found this to be a good thing, because I'm quite the opposite. I'm a bit of an abrasive personality, an acquired taste, if you will. I'm describing us in our extremes because marriage is a place where you test the extreme edges of your boundaries. For most of us, in our work or social lives, we never really get to the edges of our personalities or to our dark sides because those arenas don't push as hard on our souls. But in marriage we can get there often. Something about the complementary yet opposing character traits in most marriages combined with varying wills and visions causes us to back into our corners and lean into what feels most natural.

One embarrassing area was tested to the outer limits on many occasions, forcing Wynter to eventually become even more passive. It also caused me to become harsh and uncompromising. I will completely own this issue and take responsibility for its consequences in our marriage. The truth is, at the time it owned me.

No more than a few months into our marriage, as we settled into a level of comfort with each other, Wynter made a simple request. She had noticed that, in my anxiety and constant contemplation, I bit my nails. I'm not talking about simply biting a hangnail here or there or even just biting my nails down if they were a bit long and I didn't have nail clippers. No, I'm talking about nervous and insatiable binges that ended with raw fingers and bloody cuticles. I'd picked up the habit early in life. As long as I could remember, I'd bitten my nails—at home, at school, at work. It didn't matter where.

Well, Wynter's simple request for me to stop biting my nails was met with a simple "No, thanks." I was totally uninterested in even considering her request. No one had ever challenged me in this habit—not at school, not at work, not at home. My mom didn't have a problem with it, and neither did I. Me bringing my mom into it was the first sign that I wasn't thinking clearly. In my mind, Wynter was going to have to simply put up with it.

My denial of her request didn't seem to get much push back early on, but over time, and I mean real time—like five years—the requests came more often and with much more emotion.

Then I started noticing Wynter didn't want to hold my hand on many occasions. Without even observing closely, she knew the condition of my fingers. The grosser they were to her, the more she would decline the simple and intimate act of holding hands. Her decision to withdraw in this way seemed extreme to me. I took it as a personal rejection of me as an individual, forgetting my rejection of her request. Mostly, though, she presented her lack of support for my habit as sadness. What I didn't realize at the time, but now I see with glaring clarity, is that although Wynter despised my nail-biting, the real pain came because of the lack of care and compassion I felt for her in my decision to keep on biting.

The most heated arguments about my nail-biting came when my habit affected others. It started with me leaving bloodstains on our new white sheets, and it progressed to the reality of at least two of our daughters picking up on my habit and becoming extreme nail-biters themselves. As small of a dilemma as this may seem to you, this was an incredible barrier to sustained intimacy in our home.

Well, I'm embarrassed to say it, but it was another few years before I decided to honor Wynter's request. Seeing my daughters indulge, to the disappointment of their mother, opened my eyes to the consequence of my decision to carry on a habit regardless of my spouse's desires.

I decided to finally change my thinking. I was going to move past my history and repent of the sin of indifference toward my wife. It was the beginning of a shift to an altogether different mind-set.

There was just one slight problem: I was powerless to make the necessary change.

Nail-biting had been so engrained in my life and mind that it was a part of who I was. It wasn't something I could just put on and take off. The more I tried to stop biting my nails, the more impossible it felt to accomplish.

I heard all the stats about habit creation and knew most experts say it takes 30 days of sobriety to change a habit, but I couldn't muster the strength to make it 5 days, let alone 30. I tried to grit it out. I tried the nasty-tasting nail polish, and I even tried to wear gloves around the house and in the car. Nothing worked for long, and eventually I went right back to my old habit, like during a long car ride while deep in thought, or when I was nervous about a project. Then I'd fall back into my old ways, which led us back to a place of broken intimacy.

I spent years on a perpetual cycle of sobriety and relapse. I don't mean to make light of these terms, but the addiction I had to my nail-biting seemed no different than an alcoholic's addiction to alcohol. And though the results weren't as devastating on my family as alcohol addiction, the habit and the perception of my lack of care had a significant effect on our intimacy. It was absolutely embarrassing.

Thankfully, I reached a breaking point one day, when I reached the end of myself. I realized I was asking my wife to change some things about her, but she wasn't responding. I was angry and a bit disheartened.

In my frustration, I went to the Lord in prayer and asked Him to change Wynter. Instead He reminded me of a Scripture I knew well and asked me if I was willing to change myself. He flipped the script on me! The passage of Scripture is Matthew 7:1-5:

> Judge not, that you be not judged. For with the judgment you pronounce you will be judged, and with the measure you use it will be measured to you. Why do you see the speck that is in your brother's eye, but do not notice the log that is in your own eye? Or how can you say to your brother, "Let me take the speck out of your eye," when there is the log in your own eye? You hypocrite, first take the log out of your own eye, and then you will see clearly to take the speck out of your brother's eye.

In one moment, God reminded me of my hypocrisy and asked me to consider personal restoration. He asked me to worry about me, not Wynter. Well, I knew I had already failed at changing myself, so the only thing I knew to do was to humble myself before God, accept His will, and ask Him to change me. This prayer was a surrender and a deep shift in mind-set.

There was no 30-day plan, no nasty nail polish, no program. God, in all His power, gave me a hunger to quit I'd never had before, an awareness in the daily addiction that I had never experienced, and a power that seemed altogether foreign. Just recently I placed my hand on Wynter's thigh as we were driving, and she placed her hand gently on top of mine along with a soft squeeze. It may not seem like a big deal to you, but it reminded me that what is impossible to us is an easy fix for God.

> I realize the greatest thing standing between me
> and greater intimacy with my wife has
> been my desire to control.

As I look back over this seemingly simple yet long-term issue in my marriage, I realize the greatest thing standing between me and greater intimacy with my wife has been my desire to control. I was crippled by my own mind-set. My lack of empathy. My pride. My willingness to walk in disobedience.

In my identity with Christ in my mind, with His empathy and my humility and obedience, He sent me help. It wasn't my action, but my surrender. As I surrendered, God took over, filling me with an altogether different controlling agent, and everything changed.

My nail-biting was only one example of fleshly control, and my bloody cuticles were one of the simpler consequences.

Let me give you another example that might resonate. Though I know the Bible tells me to "turn the other cheek," in the early days of marriage, I much preferred to mentally and emotionally push back. Submission and vulnerability were not at the top of my list of priorities. I didn't feel as if I was doing anything wrong, and listening to Wynter correct me or tell me she was offended by something I did was unacceptable. Defensiveness was my number one weapon, and I knew how to wield its power. Having grown up in a home with many voices, seven people in all, I learned how to become the loudest voice. Though I couldn't quiet my siblings, ratcheting up my voice ensured that I could at least silence their voices in my head. I did this growing up, and I brought it into marriage.

When Wynter told me I hurt her feelings or asked me to stop doing this or do that, I began my race to the top of the verbal ladder in a somewhat subconscious effort to change her mind. It was manipulative and controlling, even though it felt much like a norm for me. Her concerns were an overreaction in my mind. and I completely justified my actions.

Self-control. Self-governance. I had little interest in handing the keys of my life to another controlling agent, and I still do at times. I much prefer holding on to my own need for rightness and my own position on any and every matter.

Of course, this doesn't end well. It typically ended in an argument or with Wynter turning toward indifference. Just like my nail-biting, defensiveness was a habit that needed to go!

Wynter

As I read Jonathan's words describing our nail-biting journey, all I can think is *Wow, what a brat!* And, yes, I'm referring to myself. While Jonathan graciously owns his part, I think it's only fair for me to own mine.

It's true that I wanted him to stop biting his nails for many years.

While this began as a sincere and simple request, it became the barometer by which I measured my husband's love for me. Regardless of the hundreds of other adjustments and points of growth in our relationship, his refusal to address this issue caused me to become resentful, demanding, and bratty. I wanted him to stop biting his nails for the obvious reasons he mentioned, but the longer this battle lasted, the less it became about bloody stains and the more it became about my desire to control. My request had little to do with my concern for him, but rather my desire to get what I wanted. Over the years this entire ordeal revealed how selfish, self-serving, and spoiled I really am.

I like to have things my way. All of us do, of course—some of us just handle it better when we don't get it. I am not one of those people. I am the one who cries, pleads, begs, and stomps. From the time I was a little girl, if I cried hard enough, eventually whatever I was asking for would show up at my door or in my hand. I often joke with my mother that I needed a little more "rod" in my life as a child! I don't fault her, but saying no is not one of her strong suits, and it didn't take long for me to take advantage of that. My mother loves big and selflessly, and when I was a child, that translated into her saying yes to my every request, even when what I really needed was a reality check.

Marriage has served as just that—a reality check.

I have never doubted Jonathan's love for me, yet somehow I allowed the Enemy to use this nail-biting habit to create a growing wedge between my husband and me. Funny thing is that I was fighting for control, while not realizing I was being controlled. Annoyance grew into sadness, sadness grew into distance, and that distance created feelings of resentment and ultimately a sense of betrayal.

Now, while I believe parts of each of our personalities (good or bad) can be traced back to our childhoods, what it comes down to is our nature. The Bible is clear that we are all born with a propensity toward sin, so please know that in no way am I blaming or excusing my selfishness on the selflessness of my mother! The Enemy knows our weakness, and if we're not careful, he eases his way into our lives and our marriages through unaddressed areas of sin. I truly cannot explain how silly it feels to read about the deep issues this one little habit caused.

> **God has brought my need to get my way to the surface, and its roots are not as deep as they used to be.**

Jonathan has had a few relapses, but I cannot deny the change he's experienced in his mind. The relapses have become few and further between. The habit doesn't seem so deeply engrained anymore, and I can credit that only to God's power all these years later. In the same way, God has brought my need to get my way to the surface, and its roots are not as deep as they used to be. God's Holy Spirit has sent the help we both have needed for this area, and He continues to be a very present help in time of need.

Help. We all need it. But coming to a place of asking for it or admitting we need it requires a level of humility, honesty, and acknowledgment that we can't make it on our own.

Early in our marriage we needed help, and we still do today. In those early days, we were desperate for God's help, but one specific thing was in the way of His help:

Our flesh. Our perspective. Our own governance.

Though we both had a relationship with God in Jesus, we both were still holding on to control. We were doing exactly what is spoken of in Romans 8:5: "Those who are according to the flesh set their minds on the things of the flesh, but those who are according to the Spirit, the things of the Spirit" (NASB).

Though we were born again and filled with the Spirit, we were still choosing to live as if we were the masters of our own destiny. We were living according to our flesh. In other words, we were preferring what felt natural to us, not out of any anger or resentment, but because that is how we had always done things.

We were used to our own governance. We were used to independence. Yes, we were completely surrendered to the will of God in some areas of our lives, but we had to lean into God's power anew in our marriage.

Even after giving our lives to Christ and having the Holy Spirit present in our lives, most of us—really, all of us—prefer to hold on to the reins of our lives. We prefer our own governance because we've learned to rely on ourselves, in our flesh. This is natural, especially as it relates to entering into a union with someone else, because it's the first time in our lives that we're forced into a proximity that's way too close for comfort!

It becomes easy to stop trusting God and start questioning Him. You wonder if the person you thought you married is the same person you moved in with! Rather than trust God's timing and plan, most of us run for our corners and dig in our heels, trusting instead our instincts and natural tendencies.

For us, the proximity to each other in marriage and an

understanding that our own tendencies, instincts, and controls were not enough to make our individual *me* turn into *we* forced a decision.

Thankfully, we knew Romans 8:5 well. We both knew a shift in our trusted source was necessary if we were ever going to find victory and find our *we*. We needed to live in a constant place of the "things of the Spirit."

As we look back over our years together, we see we had no one single breaking point along the way, but micro breaking points that have added up and continue to add up.

Take, for example, our children. Our first daughter was born within our first eleven months of marriage. This was a significant breaking point for us. We moved into responsibility and adulthood that caused us to truly reflect on our own growth. We thought, *If we're going to parent, we need to be growing some things in ourselves.* After all, you have to practice what you preach. After our first daughter, came three more daughters, all within the span of three years. The last two are twins, and the age difference between our oldest and youngest is only five years.

Our girls were a large dose of reality and an easy reminder that we were in desperate need. But on any given day, we also had to deal with several tensions in our marriage—past relationships, habits, trust issues, and various other battles. We were forced into either living with them or giving them to God.

We haven't always done it perfectly, but we've routinely practiced the habit of giving each of those tensions to God. We have relied on the fact that God can be trusted, so through many circumstances and tests, some that you've read about in this book, we began to put God to the test in our marriage. We began to ask Him to empty us of everything holding us back from His control so we could be filled with His Spirit.

We began to ask Him to remove the creature comforts, family quirks, and sin patterns from our lives that were filling us and controlling us. And we asked Him to replace those things with His Holy Spirit and His control.

We say we asked, but we mean God prompted. The day we exchanged vows and walked the aisle was our affirmation that we were opening our lives to the Holy Spirit's process of helping us let go of our *me* and refining our *we*.

Most of us expect to be a *we* when we walk the aisle, but God knows it takes a process. The Bible says, "A man shall leave his father and his mother and hold fast to his wife, and they shall become one flesh" (Genesis 2:24). If He didn't mean to imply a process, He wouldn't have said the two *shall* become one flesh. From leaving to cleaving, God knows it takes some real work to complete what He intended.

Thankfully, the work is not a work of ourselves, but one of the Spirit.

Spirit. It's a term we use often these days, but we rarely think about it deeply. Or we become confused about it, depending on our denomination or church subculture.

Let's spend a little time talking about spirit.

We humans have a spirit. The book of Genesis says God breathed it into us, and it's the very thing that separates us from the rest of the animal kingdom. While animals have limits, our existence swirls with intellect, creativity, emotions, and passions. Take one look at New York City from a bird's-eye view, Mount Rushmore in all its creativity, or the Great Wall of China.

Okay, let's bring it down to something we can relate to on a day-in and day-out basis. Listen to Bach or Céline Dion. Go to a Broadway play or visit your local arboretum. Spend some time ingesting one of these performances or creations in all its majesty and inspiration, and you will quickly remember the difference between mankind and every other species on this earth. We have God-inspired thoughts within us. Remember, we are made in God's image.

But when sin entered the world, that very God-given spirit became corrupt. We still have the ability to think, create, emote, and inspire, and we are still witnessing God's majesty through human ingenuity, but every one of these characteristics has been corrupted by our sin. Under the control of our own spirits, we all tend toward our sin nature. We think thoughts we should not. We create things within our minds that lead only to dark places. We emote in ways that don't honor God, ourselves, or others. And we have passions that lead us down the wrong roads and into lusts that destroy. Some of us have better control of our spirits than others, but left to ourselves, all our spirits are degrading.

Nothing exposes the natural patterns of our lives than life in proximity to someone else, marriage being the height of that experience.

In this state of imperfection, we're prone to turn to other spirits. From a spiritual perspective, you can sum those spirits up to the devil and all his demons. The Bible tells us that plainly in Ephesians:

> You were dead in the trespasses and sins in which you once walked, following the course of this world, following the prince of the power of the air, the spirit that is now at work in the sons of disobedience (Ephesians 2:1-2).

This works itself out in many different areas in our lives and in our marriages. The greatest force fighting your marriage and the vision God has in mind for it is not your spouse, and it's not your circumstances. It's the very real presence of the devil—the deceiver, as he is called. On the other hand, the greatest force fighting *for* your marriage and the vision God has in mind for it is the very real power of the Holy Spirit.

> **In every decision we make, we are choosing one spirit or the other, God's or Satan's.**

In every decision we make, we are choosing one spirit or the other, God's or Satan's.

You don't see the term as much anymore, but alcohol used to be referred to as "spirits." Let's use the spirit of alcohol as an example. It's clear from Scripture that God gave us alcohol for celebration. Whether at a wedding or in celebration of God's goodness, wine was made good. But many of us have chosen to drink wine to "relax our minds" or to find some peace or confidence we don't have. In so doing, we're looking for some other spirit to enhance our spirits. Under our spirit's control, we might take a sip hoping this spirit will give us a boost of some sort.

But how many of us know people who took this first sip to "relax their mind" and ended up under the complete control of alcohol? What can start as a pursuit of a "better spirit" can lead to total debauchery.

This control is not just with alcohol abuse. It can be seen in drug abuse. It can be seen in unhealthy eating and indulgence in food. It can be seen in excessive shopping. It can be seen in playing too much golf. The enemy of our souls and the spirit of this world—the devil—can take any created thing and use it to destroy us.

How many marriages have been ruined by all manner of habits gone awry? We have friends and family who have had their marriages ruined by alcohol, drugs, shopping, golf…Satan can even use nail-biting.

But there is good news. The same God who breathed His Spirit into every one of us at birth wants to connect with each of us through His Spirit anew. He wants to give back to us everything that has been corrupted by sin. In His perfect plan, He has created a way for us to be under the control of the only Spirit that will not disappoint—His Holy Spirit.

Jesus told His disciples of this fact, and His Word's truth reminds us of it even now. In John 16:7, He said, "I tell you the truth: it is to your advantage that I go away, for if I do not go away, the Helper will not come to you. But if I go, I will send him to you."

Some believe the Holy Spirit to be elusive, like a genie in a bottle trying not to be found. Others believe Him to be irrelevant, like a concept for Christians today to read about but not experience. Others believe He is an experience to be had as opposed to a person to know.

But He is not elusive. He is not irrelevant. And although you can experience Him, any single experience with Him cannot come close to knowing Him for yourself.

Jesus assigned to the Holy Spirit personhood, just like Him and just like the Father. And His personhood and character are described throughout the Bible.

The Holy Spirit Is Our Comforter

Have you ever met someone who makes you want to curl up in their lap? Or had a relationship with someone who just seemed to have all the right words, all the time? Well, God is described with this type of personhood.

The prophet Isaiah, encouraging anyone who looks for God in the middle of challenge and difficulty, speaks highly of this character trait of God in the Holy Spirit. Even in a book that largely casts judgment for the sins of the Israelites, God gives prophetic nuggets of hope and holiness, found only in His person. In Isaiah 40:1, the prophet begins, "'Comfort, comfort my people,' says your God."

What a way to start a chapter. A lot of chapter beginnings in the Bible might give us pause; they don't all start out as consoling as this one does. But in a book that's dark to this point, the word *comfort* brings a sweet sense of relief.

Regardless of the state of your marriage,
God promises you comfort. He promises you
sweet relief as you look to Him,
even in your darkest times.

This promise was given to the Israelites, but the truth of this Scripture still speaks to us today. Regardless of the state of your marriage, God promises you comfort. He promises you sweet relief as you look to Him, even in your darkest times.

The Israelites would face destruction and captivity, which is spoken about in the previous 39 chapters of this book. They knew they would be facing hardship because of their sin, their iniquity, and their history. Yet in this fortieth chapter begins an avalanche of messianic Scripture that speaks of the salvation, hope, and comfort found in the soon-coming king—Jesus Christ.

> See, the Sovereign LORD comes with power,
>   and he rules with a mighty arm.
> See, his reward is with him,
>   and his recompense accompanies him.
> He tends his flock like a shepherd:
>   He gathers the lambs in his arms
> and carries them close to his heart;
>   he gently leads those that have young (Isaiah 40:10-11 NIV).

The Israelites were in dark times, and you might be, as well. But consistently, God enters dark places for the sake of His people. Verse 11 tells us that the Sovereign Lord comes to guide and to gather. He comes to tend, and He comes to carry. He is gentle, and He leads.

If you feel lost or alone, He is there for you like a shepherd is for his sheep. Though the Old Testament hints of Jesus's coming, we have full knowledge of His coming as written in the New Testament. In His coming, we completely understand the fullness of God's comfort. Jesus was the one who told us exactly who that comforter is. He is the Holy Spirit.

Jesus told His disciples, "I tell you the truth: it is to your advantage that I go away, for if I do not go away, the Helper will not come to you. But if I go, I will send him to you" (John 16:7).

Many of us get a little nervous when we hear people speak of the Holy Spirit. We've either had experiences when we've thought this third person of the Trinity was superemotional and unpredictable or we think He is altogether silent and nonessential. In reality He is much more relevant than most of us have ever considered Him to be. He is relevant for our lives and relevant for our marriages.

If there's one thing all of us could use a bit more of in our relationships with our spouses, it's counseling. Thankfully, in the presence of the Holy Spirit, we can get the best counseling of our lives, and it just so happens to be free.

The Holy Spirit is described as a counselor and an advocate. He is described as a guide and a helper. He was all these things to the Israelites, and He is all these things to you. He is ready to counsel, advocate for, guide, and help. We only need to look to Him.

Wynter

I've never been a stranger to the concept of the Holy Spirit, but I can honestly say I didn't have an accurate understanding of who He is and the role He's given to play in my life as a daughter of God. As Jonathan pointed out, Scripture calls Him our help, counselor, and advocate, and my favorite identity for Him is our friend!

Jonathan and I were the first of our friends to get married. After all, our wedding was only 14 days after our college graduation. Most of our friends thought we were a little nutty for making such a huge leap into our future that soon. Although they were supportive, we found that over time, many of our friendships dissipated simply because we were on different paths.

I wouldn't say I lost my best friends, but my new lifestyle as a married woman inevitably created some distance between us. Naturally, I was focused on different things as a wife and soon after a mother. For me, at times it was lonely. I was in a new city with a new family and no friends. Yes, I had Jonathan, and he was a friend to begin with, but it was different. You see, Jonathan was born with a best friend, his identical twin brother. So although our budding and deepening friendship as a married couple was important to both of us, it wasn't as much of a priority for Jonathan because he wasn't in desperate need of a new friend. I was.

> If you've never...rested in the arms of the
> Holy Spirit while sharing the delicate details of
> your heart, then I must tell you, you're missing
> out on the best friendship ever!

At times I didn't have anyone to talk to, to cry with, or laugh with. But during these lonely and confusing days, I truly came to know and rely on the Holy Spirit as my comforter, help, and friend—not just in theory but in reality. If you've never laid back and rested in the arms of the Holy Spirit while sharing the delicate details of your heart, then I must tell you, you're missing out on the best friendship ever!

Jonathan

I'm grateful for the Holy Spirit's power, because He has overshadowed the immaturity I brought into marriage. One area where I have needed the Spirit the most is friendship. Friendship wasn't high on my list of priorities when I walked down the aisle. I didn't think friendship was bad or insignificant, but I went into marriage much more interested in intimacy, sex, and getting my needs met than seeking to be a great friend to my wife. In my mind, my twin brother had checked my friendship box.

My mind-set limited my ability to be a friend because I was more focused on me than I was on Wynter or *we*. Thankfully, the Holy Spirit has covered my immaturity and my impure motives and given me a greater desire and power to be a better friend. He has loosened some of the serious strongholds that existed in my life and were barriers to friendship as well, which I talk about in this book.

But I've also experienced the lonely place marriage can be. Some of my most disheartening times in marriage have been in times of disagreement, dysfunction, and betrayal. In those moments I've found the comfort of God. I've found Him a guide and a counselor, and His help is what I reach for anytime I find myself lost. I've found Him in the third person of the Trinity, the Holy Spirit. His presence has been as real to me in difficult times as that of any other counselor.

I remember a time when I felt all alone in marriage, and frankly, I felt betrayed. But the Holy Spirit told me I had no right to hold any sense of betrayal against my wife, because in so doing, I would be forgetting the Lord's kindness and forgiveness at my own betrayal toward Him.

> While the Holy Spirit comforts, He also convicts, and oftentimes His conviction brings the most healing.

It's funny how often counseling with the hardest advice to follow comes with the most breakthrough results. This very moment I'm sharing left me feeling angry and entitled, as if I was owed something better. But the Holy Spirit turned my thoughts toward my own issues, creating in me an altogether different view.

While the Holy Spirit comforts, He also convicts, and oftentimes His conviction brings the most healing.

Conviction. It's not a word we like to use. We like to think of convicts as those who have broken the law, and we would be right to do so. We think about those we know who are serving time in jail or are on parole after a terrible or sloppy crime.

But rarely do we like to look at ourselves as convicts. We wouldn't call ourselves convicts for the parking ticket we received last year, or for the red-light camera ticket we received in the mail. No, we reserve the term *convict* for those who have committed "big crimes." *Compared to them, I am a perfect citizen*, we tell ourselves. But all law-breakers are convicts, whether or not we like to recognize it.

At some point, we've all been convicts regarding the laws of the land, and even more so, according to Romans 3, we've been convicts from a spiritual perspective.

Jonathan

It was hard for me to comprehend this truth when I was young. Growing up in a Christian home, I learned quite well how to be a "good Christian," meaning I observed the law with a sliding scale. I didn't look at myself as a convict for running those red lights—I still don't—and I certainly didn't look at myself as a convict from a spiritual perspective. I compared myself to those who carried heavier sentences for heavier crimes.

But the longer I've lived and the longer I've been married, I've come to realize the depth of my lawbreaking. Nothing helps you see your crimes like living up close and personal with someone else. In proximity, it becomes much easier to break the law. Offense comes more naturally in proximity. And that's what the Holy Spirit comes to expose.

He comes to convict us of our sin, that we might turn from
it—from our lawlessness—and turn toward Him. In John 16:8-11,
Jesus said of the Holy Spirit, "When he comes, he will convict the
world concerning sin and righteousness and judgment: concerning
sin, because they do not believe in me; concerning righteousness,
because I go to the Father, and you will see me no longer; concerning judgment, because the ruler of this world is judged."

> In our turning toward God, His presence—His Holy
> Spirit—points us toward His truth.

In our turning toward God, His presence—His Holy Spirit—
points us toward His truth. Jesus went on to say in John 16:13,
"When the Spirit of truth comes, he will guide you into all the truth,
for he will not speak on his own authority, but whatever he hears
he will speak, and he will declare to you the things that are to come."

If you are a follower of Jesus Christ and have submitted your life
to His pruning process, His presence will be with you and guide
you toward truth. On one hand He offers comfort, but on the other
hand He offers conviction. He offers you His truth that will change
your life.

Every year of marriage for us has been a year of God exposing
sin, convicting us of those very lawless acts, and guiding us toward
His truth, toward His way. He does this gently, like a shepherd, but
also like any law officer should. He has intentions for our lives, and
His Holy Spirit won't stop short of fulfilling those intentions for
His people.

His goal is not imprisonment. While the law of the land brings
conviction for the sake of punishment, God convicts to restore. He
convicts to bring our lives closer to His truth.

Conviction is not a pleasant process, but it can lead us back to God. Thankfully, through Jesus, instead of conviction, leading to condemnation, we can choose His grace. When we welcome His grace, we welcome Him. When we welcome Him, we welcome His Spirit. Galatians 5:22-23 says, "The fruit of the Spirit is love, joy, peace, patience, kindness, goodness, faithfulness, gentleness, self-control; against such things there is no law."

While we would prefer certain characteristics not be on our resumes or in our homes, we should be happy to accept what Christ offers here both in ourselves and in our spouses.

- *Love.* Who doesn't want to feel as if their needs are at the center of their spouse's priorities?

- *Joy.* Seeing our spouse smile and filled with delight would make most of us shine right back.

- *Peace.* Harmony for most of us can be elusive, but when we recognize it in the life of another couple we know, we desperately wish we could have it ourselves.

- *Patience.* Knowing that our spouse is willing to pause to consider their judgments, comments, and conclusions would make every one of us feel more accepted and considered.

- *Kindness.* Benevolence makes us want to reciprocate that same characteristic with those closest to us.

- *Goodness.* We would be foolish to turn down this virtue in our closest relationship. With it, we can trust that our best interests are always at the top of our spouse's list.

- *Gentleness.* How many situations, arguments, and battles could be avoided if our spouse was always tender and calm?

How much chaos could we avoid if we chose to live in a way that considers and understands our spouse?

- *Faithfulness.* This is definitely a virtue we want in our spouses, and it speaks to the consistency with which they apply all these other characteristics. It's fuel for the journey.

- *Self-control.* We could all benefit if our spouses lived lives of discipline and restraint. And we would be better spouses if we lived the same way.

Scripture says no rules against living with these characteristics that come directly from God exist. Why? Because attitudes, thoughts, and actions that reflect these fruits leads only to more of the same.

In the pages ahead we'll explore where we find the power to live in such a way.

Your Turn

Sometimes we can be hard on ourselves, and it can be easy to point out all the bad fruit and characteristics we know we need removed from our marriages. But let's forget about those and dream for a second. What are some Holy Spirit fruits that seem so far out of your reach right now that you can only dream about being filled with them? Now ask God to blow your mind and fill you with these good fruits!

Prayer

Heavenly Father, many of the fruits of Your Spirit that Jesus walked with in ease seem far from my life right now. I desperately desire each of them, but I don't possess the ability to walk in them consistently or authentically in my own strength. Lord, begin a work in my life that will value these fruits more and more and give me a heart-level desire to seek You for them. Blow my mind and make me more like You. In Jesus's name, amen.

9

Power

Wynter

If we were to sit down with you and exchange the details of our marriages and seasons of marital stress, I think we'd have a lot in common. The stories might be different, but many of the challenges would be the same. I also think you have the same desire for marital bliss and happily ever afters we have.

One thing I know for sure is that your questions are the same as ours.

How do we move forward?

How can I forgive him [or her] for this?

How will I ever get my needs met?

How can I be a better spouse?

There is nothing wrong with these questions, and we encourage you to ask them. But we can assure you there is only one answer—the Holy Spirit. The same comforter mentioned in Isaiah and the same judge mentioned in John is available to you.

But I have even better news.

The same power that allowed Jesus to suffer, die, and empty Himself for us all and then raised Him from the dead is available to you.

Remember, Jesus was a man as well as God. He needed to access the Spirit's power the same as you and I do. Romans 8:11 tells us, "If the Spirit of him who raised Jesus from the dead is living in you, he who raised Christ from the dead will also give life to your mortal bodies because of his Spirit who lives in you" (NIV).

Accessing the Holy Spirit comes with an incredible ability to live a life full of power and hope that you can never have on your own.

Jonathan

One day my daughters and I were discussing our cars. My oldest daughter was doing what kids do when she began to share what she expected in her first car. She was 13 years old, and her desires weren't necessarily coming through as I would have preferred.

As she laid out her agenda, I soon realized she took the major advancements in automobile technology for granted. That reaction was a bit extreme, maybe, but sensing a level of entitlement in her spirit, I leaned back and began to break down what life with a car was like when I was her age. I wanted to give her a bit of perspective and to maybe reset her young mind.

I took her back to my 1989 Toyota Corolla! Yes, that's the car I used to pick up Wynter for our very first date.

I can still feel the red cloth seats on my back, and I should, because the air conditioner was more like a fan blowing hot summer air than the coolant systems that exist today. Instead of attempting to cool my car with my air conditioner, I preferred to wind down my windows and drive fast, allowing the hot air to bring some level of cooling inside my car and to my body. The faster I drove, the better it felt. It was all up to me.

Let's not gloss over a phrase I just used that my daughter literally didn't have in her vocabulary as it relates to cars—*wind down*. One of my younger daughters spoke up in the conversation, and said, "Daddy, what do you mean by 'wind down your windows'?" Laughing, I shared how my Corolla had no button you could push for the windows to come down, and I explained the handle I had to use, exerting much energy, to open them. They thought it was hilarious. Winding down windows was work I endured for years that they simply could not get their heads around. I even shared with them the gymnastic-like feat of trying to wind down my passenger and rear-door windows while sitting in the driver's seat—real man stuff!

Then I shared how my Corolla didn't have a built-in back-up camera. Every car my girls have experienced has had a back-up camera to assist with every difficult maneuver, and they asked me why I still sometimes stick my head out the window when I'm backing up. It's instinctive for me to do it, rotating my neck to check blind spots and ensure victory. For years I was conditioned to use this method, totally forgetting the power available to me inside my car. But in either of my cars now, I can look straight ahead at the rear camera. I can simply trust that the camera is doing its job. That's another powerful advancement my girls now take for granted.

Last, I decided to school my girls on the door technology that existed in the '80s. Since the birth of my third and fourth children, we have employed a minivan. Though they've resented every van, preferring an SUV (as has Wynter), they have totally taken for granted the ease of entry and departure from said van. All they have known is a button to open and close the van door. To demonstrate their advantage, I turned off the auto-door feature. I wanted them to learn what it feels like to have to open and close a van door with no power. For their little bodies, it's nearly impossible.

New technology requires no energy whatsoever from the driver or from the kids piling in the back. You simply engage the power, and you're good to go!

Thinking about the advancements in automotive technology is an easy way to illustrate the advancements you can have in your life and in your marriage if you simply engage the power you've been given. All the power you will ever need to live the Christian life and to grow in marriage starts with upgrading your power source. Once you've upgraded to a life with God, you simply have to engage His power.

I can continue to try to grind out an effort-filled, powerless life and marriage, or I can look to the power source given by God—the Holy Spirit.

Having thought about it, and knowing the options available to me now (although I do take pride in my old car), I would not go back to my Corolla today. Now that I've upgraded, I can continue to stick my head out the window and strain my neck to back up successfully, or I can simply look straight ahead at the rearview back-up screen. In the same way, spiritually speaking, I can continue to try to grind out an effort-filled, powerless life and marriage, or I can look to the power source given by God—the Holy Spirit.

Yes, the Holy Spirit has been given to us to comfort us in our pain, in our concern, and in our unknown. But His role is bigger than that. While He comforts, He also convicts. He convicts us of sin and even attitudes and actions that might not be sin, but that are still a barrier to where He is taking us. But although He convicts, He doesn't leave us helpless. He, the person of the Holy Spirit, is our power.

Second Peter 1:1-3 says it best when it assures us that everyone who has put their faith in Jesus Christ has been given His power:

> To those who have obtained a faith of equal standing with ours by the righteousness of our God and Savior Jesus Christ: May grace and peace be multiplied to you in the knowledge of God and of Jesus our Lord. His divine power has granted to us all things that pertain to life and godliness, through the knowledge of him who called us to his own glory and excellence.

This passage reminds us that when we receive Christ by faith, we are granted His divine power, which in turn grants us everything we need pertaining to life and godliness. I have good news: Marriage falls under the categories of life and godliness.

Wynter

I've never been a talker, but I've always been good with words. I know just how to use them to my advantage when necessary. And I am pretty good at staying silent when they are not to my advantage.

I am not a comedian, but I know timing and articulation are key when the goal is to deliver the perfect punchline with just the right amount of sarcasm! I am not an attorney, but I can talk myself out of a corner and flip the tables of guilt in a matter of seconds. I am not a counselor, but I know how to lighten a mood by adding just the right amount of humor with a slight smile. The funny thing is I've accomplished all of these with few words, but just the right ones.

Words are precious and powerful and should be handled with care. When Scripture tells us the power of life and death are in the tongue, I believe it. Proverbs 18:21 says, "Death and life are in the power of the tongue, and those who love it will eat its fruits."

I believe it, because while I say I'm good with words, I'll be honest and tell you I have not always used them for good. It's been quite the opposite, and I have had to eat its rotten fruit. Specifically, in my marriage, I've used my words to disrespect my husband, challenge his authority, and hurt his pride.

During the early years of our marriage, I became quite good at using words as a weapon. I might not have been able to be the loudest, but I knew which words would make sure I was heard loud and clear. The problem is my goal wasn't just to be heard; I wanted to hurt. I am ashamed to say that too often I succeeded. I would watch Jonathan's nostrils flare and his ego deflate because of something I said. While this gave the appearance of me winning, it never felt that way. I knew I was losing and that our marriage was suffering because of it. It was embarrassing, but no matter how hard I tried, I just could not seem to control my mouth! There were some small successes. By that I mean I held my tongue for a few minutes, but the longer the argument lasted, the more my ability to remain quiet or calm seemed impossible. Eventually a fiery sentence or two would spew out of my mouth like a lightning bolt. It was hard.

I can remember being so convicted, wanting to change, yet feeling powerless in my ability to do so. But then I asked for help.

> When harmful words escape my lips, the same Holy Spirit who convicts me also gives me the power to apologize to my husband and repent.

Now, I won't try to deceive you and make you believe I never slip. But when harmful words escape my lips, the same Holy Spirit who convicts me also gives me the power to apologize to my husband and repent.

Jonathan

One story we share with family from time to time is hilarious, and it's probably my favorite yet most humbling story to tell. We were a little beyond two years in marriage and had our first of four daughters, Alena. What's most comical about this incident is that I have no idea what we were fighting over. It obviously wasn't that significant given my memory issue. All I remember is walking out of the house into the garage while talking to Wynter with a loud voice. I won't say I was yelling, because it makes me feel better to guard against your extreme imagination.

It started with "I'm sorry I married such a close-minded person!"—an attempt for me to put her down and lift myself up. Well, it didn't work. I married a quick-witted and confident woman. Before I could even slam the door closed, she replied, "Well, I'm sorry I married a _____." I do remember the word she used. Let's just say she one-upped me, and my attempt to shut her down was met with an air strike that left me momentarily wounded! I slammed the door, retreating to my car in defeat, never forgetting my wife's ability to think on her feet!

I share this story because we laugh about it now and because it gets even more laughs from the close friends and family we tell. We were young and immature. We still are in many ways.

We fought a lot in our early days, and we're not immune to it now. I'm a highly emotional and vocal person. Wynter is a highly emotional person as well, but much less vocal. Oftentimes, in my desire to communicate, my voice and emotions build and build. This creates an emotional response in Wynter that will eventually erupt when she's ready to vocalize her emotions. This is humbling to share, except for the fact that I know you can relate!

We have grown a ton from where we once were. Back then, we didn't know how to fight the real battle—the spiritual one.

Luke 1 tells us of Mary getting the news from the angel Gabriel about her coming pregnancy. Long story short, Gabriel appears out of nowhere and tells Mary she's going to conceive a son, still as a virgin, and that she is to name Him Jesus. He goes on to tell her that Jesus is going to be a king who will rule a kingdom that will have no end, the same kingdom that was run by His forefather, David—the kingdom of Israel.

During this significant interruption to Mary's life, Gabriel calls Mary favored. He first calls her "favored one" (Luke 1:28 NASB), and then he reminds her she has "found favor with God" (verse 30 NASB). He doesn't give her a reason why she's favored; he simply clues her in on what happens to be—that God in all His wisdom has chosen to look to her for a specific task: being the conduit through which He would send a Savior and heal our world.

Overwhelmed and "perplexed" (verse 29 NASB), Mary doesn't know what to do besides ask Gabriel how she can have a child when she is a virgin. Gabriel replies with an astounding statement: "The Holy Spirit will come upon you, and the power of the Most High will overshadow you; and for that reason the holy Child shall be called the Son of God" (verse 35 NASB).

Even if you have never intently read the Bible, you might be familiar with this Scripture, if not in the New American Standard

Bible, then in another translation. It's quoted in a plethora of Christmas classics. It reads poetic and majestic, but its beauty runs much deeper than any Christmas classic or church play can convey.

That's because it speaks a truth that we all desperately need to hear and believe for our lives, that God makes His Holy Spirit—His very nature and power—"come upon you."

In our lives and in our marriages, we desperately need to know that God has the power to overshadow our lives. The imagery of God overshadowing our lives is wonderful news! It means that no matter what's going on, His very real presence is covering and overpowering anything that could be going wrong. His power can step right into a marriage you thought was dead and give it new life. His power can give birth to new dreams and an invigorated romance, and it can create a deeper level of friendship even when you were satisfied with the version you already had.

It doesn't matter where you've been or what you've done. It doesn't matter what you've brought into your marriage. The Bible doesn't give us any clue that anything innately in Mary caused God to choose her to "come upon." It just conveys the message He had for her, and that she had found His favor.

As He did with Mary, God can send His favor into your life and unleash His Spirit in your marriage in a way that can't be described as anything other than His "coming upon you."

That agent in Mary's life was the Lord. Mary was a virgin, committed to be married one day and committed to be the mother of our Lord Jesus the next. God's Spirit came upon her, and she was never the same.

The angel went on to tell Mary, "Nothing will be impossible with God" (Luke 1:37 NASB).

Mary replied with, "Behold the bondslave of the Lord; may it be done to me according to your word" (verse 38 NASB).

Mary simply received. In saying "May it be done to me according to your word," she received the news God spoke through Gabriel. And she believed God had the power to do what He said He would do.

Everything we see in this first chapter of Luke was an effort and a work of God. God granted favor. God came upon. God granted power. God overshadowed. Mary received. And God made new life out of nowhere!

You and I can have the same experience. We, too, can believe that God is offering His very same power, and receive it.

The Battle Is Spiritual

The fight in marriage—the conflict, the tension, the thing standing in the way between the marriage you know you're supposed to have and where you are now—is not physical or emotional, but spiritual. Because the fight is spiritual, victory can seem elusive. That's probably what frustrates us the most about marriage. It's difficult. It's work. It's a contact sport, but one in which the Enemy is difficult to find. Not many enter the ring and go unscathed by the sport of it.

Marriage brings you into a battle known as spiritual warfare. You might not be familiar with this concept, so allow us to explain.

In Ephesians 6:12 we're reminded of the battle we face as believers in Jesus Christ: "We do not wrestle against flesh and blood, but against the rulers, against the authorities, against the cosmic powers over this present darkness, against the spiritual forces of evil in the heavenly places."

This verse isn't talking about marriage specifically, but it absolutely includes marriage. It's speaking about our conflict with people and against life's struggles. Conflict happens only between those in proximity, and it is circumstantial. Can you think of a person you are closer to than your spouse? And can you think of times of great conflict that don't come based on difficult circumstances? In its closeness, your marriage relationship lends itself to the greatest potential for conflict.

Ephesians 6:12 reminds us that, though they feel physical and personal, our conflicts in marriage aren't with our spouses or even with circumstances we're facing. The verse tells us we're in conflict with the authorities and powers of a dark world, which are under the control of the Evil One. That's right. The Enemy of our souls is waging war against every one of us, and one of his go-to strategies is weaponizing marriage.

This is an easy truth to forget or miss. In our most heated exchanges, we both feel much in conflict with each other. It doesn't seem like some far off, spiritual, or otherworldly battle. Nope, it feels personal and earthly!

Unfortunately, some of our most memorable moments in marriage have been imprinted on our minds because of the levels of intensity and emotions that have come with them. They include heated exchanges and stark differences in opinion.

I want to spend a holiday here, and she prefers to spend it there.

I want to spend the extra dollars this way, and he wants to spend them that way.

We're reminded of a scene in the movie *War Room*, a film our oldest daughter stars in. It's a story of marriage being fought for the right way and from the right perspective.

In the movie, Alena's character's name is Danielle. The plot has to do with Danielle's mom, Elizabeth (played by Priscilla Shirer), and dad having relational issues and needing help. An older woman named Ms. Clara befriends Elizabeth and begins to mentor her.

In describing the relationship issues in her and her husband Tony's embattled marriage, Elizabeth says to Ms. Clara, "If there's one thing we do well, it's fight."

Miss Clara responds with one of the most game-changing lines in the movie when she says, "No, I don't think you do. Just because you argue a lot doesn't mean you fight well. I bet you never feel like you've won."

This short scene and dialogue quickly explain the difference between the way many of us see marital challenges and the way God sees them. It's the difference between what we know to be true in the Christian faith and how a world void of God's wisdom interprets how to win in marriage.

Godless thoughts say, *It's you against me* or *It's me against the world.* They say, *For me to win, someone else must lose* and *I'm going to fight until the winner is determined.* Boiled all the way down, it's translated, *I win when my spouse loses.*

This is not a phrase many would vocalize, but it's the reality many live. It's been true for us in varying and thankfully deflating degrees as we continue this journey and learn what it looks like to fight well.

Fighting well starts with looking at your problems in marriage through spiritual eyes. That doesn't mean ignoring the physical or emotional reality, but it does mean prioritizing and making the main thing the main thing. Key to success is learning to see and understand what is happening spiritually, recognizing there is a battle much greater than the details you're disagreeing about or the circumstances you're facing with opposite perspectives.

It's believing the truth of 1 Peter 5:6-9:

Humble yourselves, therefore, under God's mighty hand, that he may lift you up in due time. Cast all your anxiety on him because he cares for you. Be alert and of sober mind. Your enemy the devil prowls around like a roaring lion looking for someone to devour. Resist him, standing firm in the faith, because you know that the family of believers throughout the world is undergoing the same kind of sufferings (NIV).

In the middle of this passage, Peter gives a stern warning to look out for the real enemy. He wants to remind us that though our feelings and circumstances are real, they are not the ultimate enemy. He urges us to keep in mind that the fight, no matter what it looks like or feels like, is against the enemy of our souls. And that enemy is looking to use your challenges and issues as an opportunity to swallow you up and destroy your marriage.

Fighting well and engaging in the right battles begins with humility and realizing that your marriage is not all about you.

Humility. Fighting well and engaging in the right battles begins with humility and realizing that your marriage is not all about you.

In a place of humility, we recognize that someone much greater than ourselves is fighting with and for us against the real enemy. God cares about our marriages—your marriage—immensely. He longs to be given the opportunity to fight for us as we give all our worries and anxieties to Him. What's beautiful about God is that He can do this for each of us individually, along with our spouses, because He is the God of us all.

In addition to encouraging us to stay humble and give the challenges we face to God, Peter urges us to keep our eyes open. He knows this is important through experience, and he speaks God's Word to us in this regard because he knows if we open our eyes to the truth, we'll see what's really happening beyond what feels real. He wants us to peer into the spiritual realm, where the ultimate fight is being waged for your soul, the soul of your marriage, and every other soul on which you will make an impact, including your children's.

He also tells us to be sober. To be sober is to keep your mind from being controlled by any external agent. At first glance this might seem to imply that you are ultimately responsible to be the governing agent doing the controlling, but Peter alludes to another governor, another agent. Peter is confident that the power and government to stay controlled to fight spiritual battles doesn't emanate from within us, but from Jesus Christ and our reliance on Him. Peter shares this in 1 Peter 5:10: "And the God of all grace, who called you to his eternal glory in Christ, after you have suffered a little while, will himself restore you and make you strong, firm and steadfast" (NIV).

Finally, Peter tells us to resist the Enemy by standing up with our heads held high in our faith and beliefs. Peter lived just like us, with temptation and real struggle. He wanted us to understand the battle and engage in the real fight with the real enemy in the best way possible.

Spiritual battles are not encounters we naturally know how to fight. It's much easier for us to argue about our holiday schedule or how we discipline the children than it is to recognize and consider a whole different spirit looking out for our worst interest. His only interest is to influence our lives and marriages and wreak havoc. In

John 10:10, Jesus referred to this spirit as "the thief" when He said, "The thief comes only to steal and kill and destroy."

The Enemy is looking to steal, destroy, or kill your marriage! He doesn't care which one; he will settle for any of the above, and he looks forward to your loss in any way he can effect it. That's the only reason he comes, and this is his only motivation.

But Jesus stands in stark contrast to this idea. When sharing the intent of the thief, Jesus doesn't leave us hanging and hopeless, but in the same verse offers a solution in Himself: "I came that [the world] may have life and have it abundantly." Very clearly and very simply, Jesus tells us why He came into the world. He came to give us life, joy, and abundance. He came to give us hope.

Your Turn

How have you seen the Holy Spirit's power active in your life in the past? How do you need His power in your marriage right now?

Prayer

Lord Jesus, by faith, I trust that the same power that raised You from the dead is available to me as I have put my trust in You. Will you invade my life and my marriage in a way that will be undeniable to my spouse and to the watching world? Will You bring Your Spirit's power to the deepest and darkest places in my life and marriage? May my life exude Your Spirit and Your power, bringing me all the fruits of Your Spirit along the way. In Jesus's name, amen.

Part Two

Filled

The fruit of the Spirit is love, joy, peace, patience, kindness, goodness, faithfulness, gentleness, self-control;
against such things there is no law.

GALATIANS 5:22-23

I f our marriages are going to flourish, and if our *me* is going to become
we, our minds need to focus on a few key ingredients to be added
to our lives continually. These ingredients—good fruit—aren't new;
they're as old as time itself and come from the source of life Himself,
God. We each have them in limited measure, but our ability to grow
and reproduce them is limited by our humanness. Our weaknesses—
our bad fruit—are ingredients that get in the way often, so we need to
rely on a continual supply of good fruit. That continual supply is not
innate in us.

Unfortunately, we're all used to living with the ingredients that war
against our *we*. They cause you to want to think *mostly* and sometimes

only about *me*. In your daily dumping of these bad fruits, however, you will make room for an altogether different set of ingredients. What you taste and see in your relationship with your spouse may be better than the next person's, but it will continually fall short of what God had in mind. You will need to continually dump bad fruit in exchange for good fruit.

Though these ingredients are not native to you, the source of these fruits is—namely, the Holy Spirit. If you invite His presence into your life, the ingredients innate in His Spirit will be made available to you. These fruits have the potency to change your life, grow your marriage, and expand your world. They are necessary to turn our *me* to *we* in the life-giving Spirit of God. God's Spirit is the only agent, and His power is the only source available on earth to create what God had in mind when He invented marriage in the first place.

The beautiful thing about the Holy Spirit's good fruit is that it's so nutritious for our lives and for our marriages that we can never consume too much of them. If our bad fruits were sugary sweets, they might taste good in the moment, but they'd leave us with little satisfaction and less health. The good fruits God offers are much like the physical fruits and veggies that offer us nutritional value and full satisfaction day after day. While the bad fruits will destroy, the good fruits only build up.

In this next part of the book, we're going to spend time thinking and praying about each of these ingredients made available to us by God. Working on a continual supply of good fruit might not seem so appealing at first glance, but when God grows them, you'll be more appealing to your spouse than you ever thought possible. It's easy to resist and even take for granted a spouse, but it's difficult to resist God's perfect Spirit, starting with His love.

10

Love

A remarkable saying is credited to the late Elie Wiesel, a Holocaust survivor and well-known Boston University professor: "The opposite of love is not hate, it's indifference."

Not only is this concept useful in life and marriage, but it's biblical. A few thousand years before Elie coined this phrase, the author of the book of Romans said something similar about love and about the author of love Himself, God in Christ Jesus: "God demonstrates his own love for us in this: While we were still sinners, Christ died for us" (Romans 5:8 NIV).

It's easy to assume someone doesn't love you when you know they hate you. We're sure some person in your life has hated you for one reason or another. Often this happens when someone is jealous of you or for other reasons outside your control. But in some cases, a person's hate is caused by something we've done. The person who hates us is often reacting, in many cases overreacting, to an offense they've taken from our attitudes or actions.

People have myriad ways of reacting to offense, but it normally goes one of two ways. First, they look for retribution. The worst gossip, fighting, bickering, and slandering is motivated by hate. But another reaction motivated by hate is less easily recognized, yet powerful and hurtful: indifference.

Indifference is seen in many different areas of life. If you are indifferent about your health, that might look as simple as having no discipline about what you eat or about getting normal exercise for your body. You might not say you hate your body, but the act of neglect and the road it leads to demonstrates that you don't love your body.

The way you demonstrate you have a healthy love for your body is adequately caring for it. You feed it the right foods. You get it the right amount of rest. And despite the ease of life these days, which requires only limited activity for most of us, we go out of our way to go to the gym or take a walk to get enough exercise. We demonstrate that we love our body with action. For most of us, this type of demonstration of love for our bodies isn't easy. But those of us who learn the value of loving our bodies in a healthy way realize our love will come with sacrifice.

Most of us can easily measure the result of sacrifices we make for our body. For instance, increased muscle and decreased fat are signs of your demonstration of love, as are bright and bag-less eyes and smooth and moist skin.

Demonstration. In Romans 5:8 the apostle Paul uses the word *demonstrates* when describing God's love for us. It's a simple word, but pregnant with a question: Demonstrating what?

The obvious answer is love, of course. But if you think deeper about the question, you'll begin to wonder what is meant by the word *love* here. Paul certainly isn't speaking of love in the sense our American, Western, Hollywood, and social media minds think about the word. No, he is speaking of love in action.

God demonstrated His love for us with tangible actions, just like we demonstrate the love of our own bodies with tangible actions. The demonstration of His love involved myriad sacrifices—suffering imprisonment, shaming, torture, and maligning to start. But the demonstration of His love ended with death, which was different and much more sacrificial than what we're willing to give for the love of our bodies, of course.

I love Dr. Tony Evans's description of biblical love in his book *The Kingdom Agenda*. It's so poetic, yet so simple: "The definition of love is passionately and righteously pursuing the well-being of another."

When Jesus went to the cross to demonstrate His love, He did so for the sake of righteousness. He, already being righteous, having lived a perfect life, demonstrated His love by giving us His righteous life so that we might become righteous.

Romans 5:6-8 tells us,

> You see, at just the right time, when we were still powerless, Christ died for the ungodly. Very rarely will anyone die for a righteous person, though for a good person someone might possibly dare to die. But God demonstrates his own love for us in this: While we were still sinners, Christ died for us (NIV).

Christ died for us with astonishing passion. In fact, the story of the suffering and crucifixion of Jesus is commonly referred to as "the passion," as in the movie *The Passion of the Christ*, simply because of how far God's passion drove Him on our behalf. "Passion" comes from the Greek word *pascho*, which has to do with the sense of feeling and of being affected by something.

Jesus, in His great love for us, recognized that payment for sin was required. In other words, to demonstrate His love, He would have to face a spiritually legal requirement: death for the payment of sins. That's righteousness.

But fulfilling the legal requirement would require passion. It would require a sense of feeling in a way that is difficult, almost impossible, for us to imagine. His passion led Him to go through trials we would rather never think about, let alone face.

In righteousness and passion, Jesus pursued and demonstrated His love for us.

Likewise, in righteousness and passion, we will pursue and demonstrate our love in this world and most definitely in our marriages.

> We can talk about love, and we can even
> feel "lovish," but until our love is demonstrated,
> we're just talking.

In marriage, love is demonstrated by specific, right actions, motivated out of passion for righteousness and for our spouse. We can talk about love, and we can even feel "lovish," but until our love is demonstrated, we're just talking. Our love for our spouse is measured in our actions as easily as our love for our body is measured.

Because we're believers, love is a fruit promised to us in the presence of God through the Holy Spirit. Though we have a certain amount of love in our lives by nature because we're made in God's image, the Bible tells us the only way to be filled with this fruit is through His presence.

When speaking of this fruit, the apostle John shared the greatest example of love another way—by quoting Jesus: "This is My commandment, that you love one another, just as I have loved you. Greater love has no one than this, that one lay down his life for his friends" (John 15:12-13 NASB).

John, referring to Jesus's love for us, reminds us that God, in Christ Jesus, emptied Himself of everything He had the right to hold on to, to demonstrate His love for us. He emptied Himself so that we could be filled.

What an incredible example of what our marriages should look like on a day-in and day-out basis. Most of us won't have to literally die for our spouses. But what would it look like if we had the mindset of Jesus, a willingness to love each other so tangibly that we'd lay down the silly things we hold on to, to fill up our spouses?

God's demonstrated and measurable love for us has amazing results. Romans 2:4 reminds us that His love is what draws us in: "Do you presume on the riches of his kindness and forbearance and patience, not knowing that God's kindness is meant to lead you to repentance?" (Romans 2:4).

God's love draws us to repentance. His actions—His kindness, His slowness to judge, His patience—have had a direct impact on this world, and they have caused millions upon millions to follow Jesus.

What an incredible example for us to follow—loving in a way that causes our spouses to want to repent based on our love, or to follow after us because of our willingness to sacrifice.

God's love had a single focus—the eternity of mankind.

Likewise, when we ask to be emptied of indifference, and when we ask to be refilled with God's Spirit, our love becomes singularly others focused.

We can't be emptied and refilled without God showing up.

What would our marriages look like if we asked God to make this mind-set our mind-set, and if we asked His Spirit to mold our souls? We can't be emptied and refilled without God showing up, and that's why we should all be so grateful for other scriptural reminders that tell us being others focused won't be our doing in the first place.

Paul reminds us of this very fact when he says,

> Since we have been justified by faith, we have peace with God through our Lord Jesus Christ. Through him we have also obtained access by faith into this grace in which we stand, and we rejoice in hope of the glory of God. Not only that, but we rejoice in our sufferings, knowing that suffering produces endurance, and endurance produces character, and character produces hope, and hope does not put us to shame, because God's love has been poured into our hearts through the Holy Spirit who has been given to us (Romans 5:1-5).

God helps us love our spouses as He has loved us. God causes us to lay aside our wants to serve our spouse's needs. May we continue to righteously and passionately pursue the well-being of our spouses, knowing that it's the greatest way to find love in return.

Your Turn

How have you been indifferent to your spouse? What are some new, tangible ways you can demonstrate your love that you know they'll appreciate?

Prayer

Heavenly Father, left to myself, I tend toward indifference and apathy. Through Your Holy Spirit, may You form in me a love for my spouse that is demonstrable and tangible. Create in me a passion and a righteous pursuit that will drive me to do whatever is necessary to express my love in a way that will assure my spouse of their value and worth in my eyes. In Jesus's name, amen.

11

Joy

For the joy set before him he endured the cross.

Hebrews 12:2 NIV

Martin Luther King Jr. once said, "Those who are not looking for happiness are the most likely to find it, because those who are searching forget that the surest way to be happy is to seek happiness for others."

These words were spoken by a man who leveraged his life for others. For more than a decade, he risked his life pursuing a better life and joy for an entire race of people, along with others from various backgrounds, who were subject to discrimination and desperate for hope. Motivated by a righteous indignation and a love we still marvel at all these decades later, Martin Luther King Jr.'s passionate pursuit has brought millions of people much more than happiness; it's brought them real joy.

Martin Luther King Jr. was imprisoned. He was bombed. He

was slandered. And he was eventually assassinated. He walked headlong into these circumstances because of a joy he believed would be realized ahead. He fixed his eyes on the goal, and because of his foresight, despite his death, joy came to millions and millions.

> While happiness is temporary and circumstantial, from a biblical perspective, joy is eternal and noncircumstantial.

Joy. It's much greater than happiness. While happiness is temporary and circumstantial, from a biblical perspective, joy is eternal and noncircumstantial. Though happiness can come and go, joy is promised to all those who believe and receive the gift of God in Christ Jesus.

For believers, joy is another fruit promised in the presence of God through the Holy Spirit. Though we have a certain amount of joy in our lives by nature because we're made in God's image, the Bible tells us the only way to be filled with this fruit is through God's presence.

When speaking of this fruit, the writer of Hebrews gives us a word picture that should have an impact on our lives and specifically on our marriages:

> Therefore, since we have so great a cloud of witnesses surrounding us, let us also lay aside every encumbrance and the sin which so easily entangles us, and let us run with endurance the race that is set before us, fixing our eyes on Jesus, the author and perfecter of faith, who for the joy set before Him endured the cross, despising the shame, and has sat down at the right hand of the throne of God (Hebrews 12:1-2 NASB).

This is great imagery for what we've been meditating on all along. This Scripture speaks to more than marriage, but it can be applied directly to our marriage and yours. First, each of us is running a race in our marriage, and so are you. You might be further down the road than us, or we might be further down the road than you, but every marriage is going *somewhere*.

Sadly, some marriages don't make it to the finish line or get tripped up along the way, but once the race begins, you have only a few choices. You can run fast or slow. You can get tired and begin walking. Some of us will even crawl. We've gone through all these options. Thankfully, we've never just stopped.

But the writer of Hebrews tells us to lay aside the sin and every hindrance keeping us from running with endurance. He's saying to ask the Lord to help you empty yourself of everything and anything that's weighing you down. Yes, there will be bumps and obstacles on the road, but, he says, just keep enduring, and he gives us a significant focal point and an amazing motivation.

The focal point is Jesus. The writer knows that in every proverbial race we run— marriage included—the only way we can be sure we're headed in the right direction is by keeping our eyes fixed on our Savior. By keeping our minds fixed on His promise. By keeping our souls tethered to His very presence. You see, the only way we can see Jesus is if He is present.

When we realize He is present on our route and we look to Him, His presence and Spirit change everything. The emptier we become of the sin and barriers that hinder us on the race, and the fuller we become with His Spirit, the closer we get to the prize promised in God's presence—joy.

The opposite of joy is misery, and Jesus had to put up with two miseries for His joy to be complete—the cross and shame.

Despite the misery of the cross, He endured the temporary nature of it to pay the full weight of the penalty for our sin and yours. And despite absolutely hating the shame of loneliness, abandonment, nakedness, mockery, and torture, He endured it all for us. He humbled Himself and became a servant, with you and us in mind.

You see, His endurance had only one focus, and the object of His joy was singular—the eternity of mankind.

Likewise, when we ask to be emptied and refilled with God's Spirit, our joy becomes singularly focused—others focused.

What would our marriage look like and what would your marriage look like if we asked God to make this mind-set our mind-set and asked His Spirit to mold our souls?

Once again, what would our marriages look like if we asked God to make this mind-set our mind-set, and if we asked His Spirit to mold our souls? We can't be emptied and refilled without God showing up, and that's why we should all be so grateful for other scriptural reminders that tell us being others focused won't be our doing in the first place.

As he speaks to the people, Nehemiah reminds us that even in a dark place, God's joy is found in His strength:

> Go and celebrate with a feast of rich foods and sweet drinks, and share gifts of food with people who have nothing prepared. This is a sacred day before our Lord. Don't be dejected and sad, for the joy of the Lord is your strength! (Nehemiah 8:10 NLT).

And the psalmist David reminds us as well.

> Praise the Lord!
>   For he has heard my cry for mercy.
> The Lord is my strength and shield.

I trust him with all my heart.
He helps me, and my heart is filled with joy.
I burst out in songs of thanksgiving.
The LORD gives his people strength.
He is a safe fortress for his anointed king (Psalm 28:6-8 NLT).

God helps us to endure, and God gives us joy. May you and we continue to fix our eyes on Jesus (Hebrews 12:12 NIV), the One who will bring joy beyond all circumstances and beyond everything that seeks to slow us down in our marital race.

Your Turn

In what areas of your marriage have you been seeking personal happiness over the Holy Spirit's joy? How has this negatively affected your marriage? What would it look like for you to seek joy over your own happiness?

Prayer

Lord Jesus, I've often sought quick and temporary happiness at the expense of seeking real joy. I've put myself and my needs for fulfilment ahead of Your purposes and long-term joy in my marriage. Help me to realize that happiness is often about me, while joy always takes my mate into consideration. Teach me and guide me into an endurance that is fixated on joy, knowing that it will benefit me and bless my spouse, but also bring glory to Your name. In Jesus's name, amen.

12

Peace

On separate occasions, we've both been privileged to visit Israel. Although it's only the size of New Jersey, this nation has had a substantial impact on the world and continues to export influence, goods, and a myriad of services around the globe. It is a special land with special people.

What's most interesting to notice while touring the country is the beauty and peace it experiences relative to the chaos, war, and international calamity that exist just outside its borders. It's not uncommon to see signs of war all around as you look out over some of its neighbors. Israel is surrounded by nations that would prefer it not exist and that continue trying to destroy it, yet it stands as a beacon of freedom and hope. Ironically, the greatest beacon of freedom came from within its gates. From its people, the Jewish people, the Messiah rose. And with Him came a peace for anyone who dares to walk in His ways.

I can't help but think of a psalm that brings light to this reality and its continued hope.

How blessed is everyone who fears the LORD,
Who walks in His ways.
When you shall eat of the fruit of your hands,
You will be happy and it will be well with you.
Your wife shall be like a fruitful vine
Within your house,
Your children like olive plants
Around your table.
Behold, for thus shall the man be blessed
Who fears the LORD.

The LORD bless you from Zion,
And may you see the prosperity of Jerusalem all the
days of your life.
Indeed, may you see your children's children.
Peace be upon Israel! (Psalm 128 NASB).

This psalm is a picture of what happens in the life of the person who takes God seriously, the person who fears Him. You find that God's intended end is peace when the psalmist finishes with the line "Peace be upon Israel!" but the author starts with something altogether different. He starts with the reality that this peace begins in the life of an individual who walks with God.

He then goes through a poetic set of verses that describe this person's life. He says they will be blessed. Their work, marriage, family, legacy, and finally nation will all be blessed.

It's an amazing promise and principle, but in this passage, God assigns this ultimate peace only to the person who walks with Him.

What is peace?

Peace is calm in the storm. Peace is harmony in the middle of chaos. Peace is security in peril.

Biblical peace can be summed up as harmony in
relationship with God and with others.

Biblical peace can be summed up as harmony in relationship with God and with others.

Peace in marriage is not defined by the circumstances you find yourself in. In your marriage, you will find yourself in many different circumstances you'll not prefer and that will feel like too much pressure—from the outside and from within. Many times you'll have to choose peace in your marriage when you think your spouse is causing the chaos. That's when you must realize that peace is also unity in difference. It's finding a way to find rest in your heart, even as the boat is rocking on the waves of life—and the boat will surely rock at times.

But where does peace come from? Psalm 29:11 says, "The Lord gives strength to his people; the Lord blesses his people with peace" (niv).

According to the Bible, peace comes from God. But it doesn't just come from Him; it's a blessing from Him. That's important to understand, because knowing it's a blessing reminds us peace can't be earned. We receive it as a gift.

Just as we receive Jesus, we receive His peace. The Bible says it plainly: "He himself is our peace, who has made the two groups one and has destroyed the barrier, the dividing wall of hostility" (Ephesians 2:14 niv).

In this passage, the apostle Paul is talking about the fact that in the grace and mercy of Jesus, two separate parties can be made one. He is specifically talking about how the differences between the Jews and Gentiles (all non-Jews) would be reconciled, how each party was now an equal participant in the grace of God through Jesus. He describes how both Jews and Gentiles have complete reconciliation with God, but also with one another. He even went so far as to say the two groups were now one, something unheard of in those days.

The principle of oneness for Jews and Gentiles is good news for us as Christians, and it's good news for you in your marriage. The differences between these two groups in those days were massive—much greater than any difference you might find between you and your spouse. But the hope they had to become reconciled and to be filled with peace is the same hope God offers you in your marriage. He offers you the same oneness.

For believers, peace is another fruit promised in the presence of God through the Holy Spirit. Though we have a certain amount of peace in our lives by nature because we are made in God's image, the Bible tells us the only way to be filled with this fruit is through His presence.

Ephesians 2:14 says plainly that Jesus "himself is our peace" (NIV). We don't have to guess where to find it or how to grow in it. As we look for Jesus, as we receive Jesus, and as we follow Jesus, we are promised peace in His presence.

As we ask God to empty us of all the things that keep us separate from Him, Jesus fills us with more of Himself, and by the very nature of His character, more of His peace.

What would our marriages look like if we truly believed this truth? What would our marriages feel like if we began to ask God to empty us of the things that keep us in bondage to chaos and affected by the storms, and to fill us with His presence and peace?

Jesus is called the Prince of Peace. That means He has total authority to give peace to you and your marriage.

Most of us don't think about this truth except at Christmas, but Jesus is called the Prince of Peace. That means He has total authority to give peace to you and your marriage.

Sometimes we won't feel as if this is true, and we'll simply have to take God at His Word, and meditate, memorize, and internalize all that He says about His peace. In times like these, the only thing we can do is recite simple truths as found in Philippians 4:6-7:

> Be anxious for nothing, but in everything by prayer and supplication with thanksgiving let your requests be made known to God. And the peace of God, which surpasses all comprehension, will guard your hearts and your minds in Christ Jesus (NASB).

May we be people of prayer who continually ask the Lord to empty us of those things that lead away from His peace and to fill us with His harmony and oneness.

Your Turn

How have you sought your own satisfaction in your marriage, disregarding peace? What storm has arrived or is making landfall in your marriage that you need the Holy Spirit's power to endure and experience?

Prayer

Heavenly Father, thank You that You don't just offer me a transactional peace that comes and goes, but that You offer me relationship with You and constant peace in Your presence. Forgive me for where I've sought personal satisfaction over peace, and help me to look at any storm that comes my way as an opportunity to experience Your peace, as rough as that storm might seem. I trust Your presence and wait for Your calming Spirit to take over. In Jesus's name, amen.

13

Patience

I f any idea has been lost in our microwave-, instant-gratification-, and social media-world, it's patience. In work, family, and social life, the world seems to be always pressing toward quicker, faster, and cheaper.

Gone are the days when most of us sit down to draft a beautifully handwritten letter to convey our feelings. Sometimes we're even too lazy to send a text or an email because it's so much easier to shoot a quick video. We have little time for thoughtfulness, even though our ability to express more thoughts is now so simple. We've sped up our outputs, leaving little time for mental processing. Our communications are on the surface and inauthentic. We've been conditioned to get them done quickly and efficiently.

We have even less capacity to receive with patience. We want an instant return on our online application. We want our food "right now!" We want our hotel check-in to be immediate. It doesn't matter what we're receiving, if we don't get it right away, we tend to see that as a problem.

We treat our marriages the same way. We want our spouses to respond to our needs immediately. We want them to instantly understand our feelings and process our concerns. If it doesn't happen right away, our feelings get hurt, we get angry, and at worst we abandon our post. We feel entitled doing so because that is how the rest of the world works.

No so with God. The Scriptures say it so well: "Then the LORD passed by in front of him and proclaimed, 'The LORD, the LORD God, compassionate and gracious, slow to anger, and abounding in lovingkindness and truth'" (Exodus 34:6 NASB).

The "him" in this verse is Moses. God is walking Moses through the re-creation of the stone tablets with the Ten Commandments, His law the Jews were to live by. Moses had seen these words when they were etched the first time. We can only imagine that even Moses was intimidated by the weightiness of each commandment as he etched them into the tablets.

Take, for example, murder. When he came across the commandment that says you shouldn't murder, he had to remember that he was a murderer. How intimidating would that have been? But in the middle of this process God made this amazing statement about His compassion, His grace, His slowness to become angry, and His abounding loving-kindness and truth. It had to have put Moses at ease to hear these words as the law was laid out, law he certainly was not even worthy to write down.

God was conveying His patience for His people, including Moses. He was reminding them that, even in His expectations, there would always be grace and mercy. He was giving a sign of what marriage would be like between Him and His people, Israel. After all, God would describe Israel as His bride and Himself as their groom:

Your Maker is your husband—
   the Lord Almighty is his name—
the Holy One of Israel is your Redeemer;
   he is called the God of all the earth (Isaiah 54:5 NIV).

In their symbolic marital relationship, God promised many things, but none more important than His patience. His patience would get them to a place of receiving His law. His patience would create the Old Testament sacrificial system. And His patience would decide to come to earth as the God-Man to demonstrate His astounding love for mankind.

After accomplishing salvation for mankind, God promised to return to judge those who refuse Him. But even in this final act, He promised patience. Second Peter 3:8 says, "Do not let this one fact escape your notice, beloved, that with the Lord one day is like a thousand years, and a thousand years like one day" (NASB).

Imagine God saying here, "I can put up with a thousand years of waiting and watching you mess up time after time if it means bringing you home." Or imagine Him saying, "I love you so much that a thousand years feels like only a day, because My commitment to you is so rock-solid."

Now imagine having this same type of commitment toward your spouse. Imagine having this type of patience that would cause you to not only be willing to wait, but to express that level of communication toward your spouse in any area of your relationship where you would prefer to cast judgment.

Unfortunately, we do not have the same level of patience God has when it comes to our relationship with each other in marriage.

Unfortunately, we do not have the same level of patience God has when it comes to our relationship with each other in marriage. We are much quicker to pass judgment for acts of treason that should have far lesser sentences than the one we would owe God should He act in judgment.

Thankfully, the same Holy Spirit that grants us love, joy, and peace willingly grants us the very Christlike patience Moses experienced while etching the tablets and that we all received through the slow and torturous death of Jesus.

For believers, patience is another fruit promised to us in the presence of God through the Holy Spirit. Though we have a certain amount of patience in our lives by nature because we're made in God's image, the Bible tells us the only way to be filled with this fruit is through His presence: "Consider it all joy, my brethren, when you encounter various trials, knowing that the testing of your faith produces endurance. And let endurance have its perfect result, so that you may be perfect and complete, lacking in nothing" (James 1:2-4 NASB).

In our relationships with our spouses, we each need to reset our minds and our perception about what is happening. James, the brother of Jesus, tells us God uses some of the trials we go through in life to test our faith and create endurance and patience in us. We say *some*, but it sounds like *all*, because James says consider it "all" joy, meaning that even if a trial couldn't possibly seem as if it is coming from God, act as if it is, knowing that God is growing you through it!

May we ask the Lord to empty us of any perception we have of being right to see growth in our marriages. May we be filled with His Spirit of patience so we can patiently endure the trials God uses in our marriages to make us complete and perfect.

Your Turn

What challenges in your marriage have you wanted to rush through? What do you think God could be wanting to grow in you? How can your patience in this area bring about God's best for your relationship with your spouse?

Prayer

Lord Jesus, far too often I find myself quick to judge and quick to assign punishment to my spouse, while at the same time expecting perfect patience from them and from You in my struggles. Forgive my hypocrisy in this area. Teach me the value of patience, and help me to view my patience as an act of love and affection toward my spouse. May the patience You give me through Your Holy Spirit be a key to unlocking the type of response I'm hoping to see, and that I know will not come from my impatience. In Jesus's name, amen.

14

Kindness

Wynter

We have a dog. Well, we have a Yorkie-poo. There's a difference. Nothing against those of you who have other types of dogs, but something about our boy Max is just a little special. Just a bit more human. He's also intelligent, incredibly loving, and the perfect size.

He's not as small as most Yorkie-poos; most are five or so pounds. He's double that size, weighing in at more than ten pounds on his good days. He also has a gorgeous coat of silky black curls. Our girls get a kick out of the fact that his curls closely resemble Jonathan's. If they lie side by side, with Max near Jonathan's head, you almost can't tell the difference between them. They do lie side by side often, as Max helps Jonathan and all of us, as first-time dog owners and lovers, realize a dog really is man's best friend.

His friendship runs deep. To our girls, he's become a big brother. He takes on the personality of a protector at night when they're fast asleep in their bedrooms. He typically lies on the edge of one of their beds, only moving if he hears the slightest, faint sound that might be an intruder or would-be burglar. He jumps up, runs to the middle of the house, and begins to bark, growl, and make his presence known.

In his mind, he's a German shepherd, but if you were to come to our house and view this scene, you wouldn't be able to help smiling and chuckling at the cuteness of it all.

Max is also loyal and as sweet as a dog can be. He loves to be close, and he loves attention. In our eyes, he's perfect. We see only his value, and from this frame of reference, he can do no wrong. And because of that, our kindness to him knows no end.

It's not that he does no wrong in reality; he absolutely does. His bark is high pitched, and on many days, it cuts through the air and into your ears like a siren. It can be annoying, especially on a day when you just want to rest. He also rings a bell we have on the door when he wants to go outside. He's supposed to use it only when he wants to go to the bathroom, but he typically takes advantage of our kindness and rings the bell far more often than his bladder requires. This can be inconvenient and frustrating. He goes through seasons when he forgets that our wood floors are not his bathroom. It's not often, but when it happens, it makes me want to scream! He eats our shoes and the girls' toys, and recently he's been finding his way on top of the kitchen table. Come to think of it, his wrong could fill a notebook.

But though I go through moments of frustration with him, in the end I don't remember them. I revert to kindness. There's just something about my relationship with him that forces me to look on him with compassion and kindheartedness. I can get angry with him for a moment, but over the course of his short life, my kindness and the kindness of my family has prevailed. Much Max has done in deed has deserved anything but kindness, but we continue to love him, save him from himself when he wants to attack a dog three times his size, and be merciful when he eats yet another valuable item in our home.

Surprisingly, having Max has taught me much about the kindness of God. I have always known His kindness theoretically, but owning this cute, curly-headed pup has taught me much experientially. Titus 3:4-5 says, "When the kindness of God our Savior and His love for mankind appeared, He saved us, not on the basis of deeds which we have done in righteousness, but according to His mercy, by the washing of regeneration and renewing by the Holy Spirit" (NASB).

Jesus emptied Himself and appeared on the scene out of kindness. He came for His sheep, as He calls us. Sheep are an even less sophisticated animal group than the one Max comes from. Motivated by His love, offering us peace and joy, in His great patience He came to lavish us with His kindness. His kindness isn't based on anything we've done right, but just on His mercy.

In His mercy He has forgotten what we have done and lavished us with compassion, so that He might wash us and make us new by His Holy Spirit!

Unfortunately, the kindness God has offered us and the kindness many of us bestow on our pups and pets can be easily forgotten when it comes to our spouses. In our marriage relationships we have all been guilty of quickly reciprocating our spouse's lack of kindness or deed done in selfishness with a grander lack of kindness or a worse deed.

I wish I could say Jonathan and I have perfected kindness, but we have not. Yet as we've submitted our lives to God individually, and as we've submitted our marriage to the Holy Spirit's power, God has given us increasing compassion and kindness that didn't exist in our earliest days of marriage.

> As we've begun to live out the Holy Spirit's kindness to each other, we've noticed our kindness affects the other's ability to be kind.

As we've begun to live out the Holy Spirit's kindness to each other, we've noticed our kindness affects the other's ability to be kind. This shouldn't surprise us, because Scripture speaks to this reality from an eternal perspective and gives us an even better example of what kindness can do: "Do you think lightly of the riches of His kindness and tolerance and patience, not knowing that the kindness of God leads you to repentance?" (Romans 2:4 NASB).

The kindness of the Holy Spirit and God's power gave Jesus the strength to do what He did. His kindness has led us back to Him. In emulating Jesus, we can walk with the same power and the same kindness He did. The same Holy Spirit that grants love, joy, peace, and patience willingly grants us Christlike kindness.

For believers, kindness is another fruit promised in the presence of God through the Holy Spirit. Though we have a certain amount of kindness in our lives by nature because we're made in God's image, the Bible tells us the only way to be filled with this fruit is through His presence.

Your kindness toward your spouse can have a significant effect on your marriage and be an important tool of healing. God can use this fruit in your life to save you from a fight and even a season of bitterness and distance.

May we all be people who ask God to empty us of the need to reciprocate unkindness, deed for deed. May we be people who ask

God for more of His power and presence to be kind, so our marriages will be better for it. May we be people who wash our marriages with the compassion and kindness that comes only from the power of the Holy Spirit.

Your Turn

Does your spouse have an attribute or has taken a specific action you can't stop thinking about? What would your compassion in this area do for your marriage should you decide to release what you're holding? What would your unmerited kindness mean to your spouse?

Prayer

Heavenly Father, on most days I forget about Your kindness. I take it for granted, and I assume its presence. But when I'm reminded of Your great kindness for me, I can't help but feel grateful, even special. May this same kindness I've received from You be the kindness I pass on to my spouse through Your Spirit's power. Enable me to walk with a supernatural kindness that will cause my spouse to mistake me for You. May our kindness to each other be a bridge of grace in time of need. In Jesus's name, amen.

15

Goodness

Many attitudes, habits, and patterns have needed to change in our marriage over the years, and they have. But because of the nature of our humanity, they always exist.

No matter if it's a desire to get our way, an uncontrollable habit our spouse doesn't prefer, or an attitude of self-righteousness, if we want to change, motivation must be added to the mix.

We all have motivation for everything we do, a reason behind every thought and every act. Oftentimes the thought behind the act causes the fight or tears. We can say the exact same phrase to our spouse at two separate times, yet get totally opposite reactions. That's because as humans we tend to look past what's said to the heart. We want to look at and understand the motivation behind the words, and on many occasions our hearts aren't good. Our motivations can be rotten.

This often causes conflict, worry, fear, and concern, because as flawed people, our motivations shift. They don't remain consistently good and can tend to leave an uneasiness and lack of assurance in the mind of our spouse.

Not so with God.

Jonathan

If you were to ask me to tell my story of turning toward Jesus, you wouldn't get an elaborate "I once was lost, but now I'm found." It's not that I wasn't lost, and it's not that I wasn't found; it's just that when I look back over my life, I don't remember a time when I didn't know God. I can remember times when I rebelled against His commands, and I can remember times when I questioned my love for Him, but I've never questioned His motivation. His goodness. His love for me. I knew it from my earliest days.

You see, my testimony is easily summed up and can be extracted from Psalm 34:8: "Taste and see that the LORD is good; blessed is the one who takes refuge in him" (NIV).

I've had the opportunity to test and taste God's goodness because it has been served up for me plentifully with all its various fruitful flavors. For starters, my parents showed me an incredible display of God's goodness, as did a host of other family, friends, and church members.

Even in the difficult, bad, and ugly, I've had the opportunity to experience God's virtuousness. In the death of relatives and friends, I've seen His consistent hand of love.

In my darkest days, His goodness has given me peace, resolve, and hope. And so, as the psalm encourages us to do, I've made Him my refuge. I've made Him—or received in Him—a fortress.

In Him I consistently find my dwelling, my peace, my protection, my provision, and life itself. I have no worries that He won't be all that, because it's who He is and what He does. Through every circumstance and through every season of life, that's just who He is.

God's singular inspiration is His goodness. It's His sole frame of reference. It's His motivation for all that He does. In His grace, mercy, judgments, and restraints, He is coming from a place of goodness.

God's goodness motivated Him to create a plan to rescue us from disaster. His goodness motivated Him to leave perfection to enter an imperfect world. That same goodness stirred Him to an active plan of emptying Himself of everything He had to fill us up. His goodness sent His Holy Spirit we can call on today. His goodness is a daily reminder that He has our best interests in mind.

That is a difficult concept for many of us to believe because we haven't seen that goodness from others. We tend to look at the world through eyeglasses that filter what we see through our experiences. That holds true in our marriages as well.

Each one of us is desperate for a marriage where goodness is a foundation. Whether or not we know, having goodness as a foundation shores up the cracks and braces for the times when the winds swell and the storms rage.

We long for consistency and goodness in our spouses,
and if we find them, they will be our
greatest tools for building trust.

We long for consistency and goodness in our spouses, and if we find them, they will be our greatest tools for building trust.

Yet if any of the fruits God offers us seem impossible to conjure up, goodness is the one! They're all impossible to conjure up, but this one can be the most difficult. That's because, while all the other fruits seem above the surface, this one sits just below it. Goodness seems more of an impulse than an action or a manageable characteristic.

Thankfully, the same Holy Spirit that grants love, joy, peace, patience, and kindness willingly grants us Christlike goodness as well.

For believers, goodness is another fruit promised in the presence of God through the Holy Spirit. Though we have a certain amount of goodness in our lives by nature because we're made in God's image, the Bible tells us the only way to be filled with this fruit is through His presence.

How different would our marriages be if we could trust that at the very core of our motivation is the Spirit's goodness? How much safer would we feel if we could trust that God is imparting to each of us a below-the-surface urgency and impulse to operate from a place of having each other's best interests in mind?

May we continually ask God for a power that shifts our motivation at its very core. May His power cause in us a consistent spirit and aspiration for goodness for each other. And may His Spirit lead us to a deeper level of trust and dependency on each other, just like we can have in Jesus Christ.

Your Turn

What is your motivation in your marriage? When you're planning and reacting, what are you hoping to accomplish? Take some time to meditate on whether goodness is at the core of your motivation.

Prayer

Lord Jesus, as Scripture reminds me, I confess You are good and Your mercy endures forever. I never have to question this reality, because its truth is as true as anything I know to be true. May Your goodness supernaturally abound in me, and may the very goodness that led You to the cross rise in me. May the same power that lived in You be alive in me, causing a goodness that results in actions and attitudes that bring my spouse assurance of my love and faithfulness. In Jesus's name, amen.

16

Faithfulness

Jonathan

I recently attended the funeral for a giant in the faith whose life and work mattered much in the kingdom of heaven. Dennis Keith Forster, a native of South Africa and a man who committed his life to serve Jesus Christ at a very young age, gave his entire life, commitment, and passion in the faithful pursuit of making the Bible readily available to unreached people groups around the world. Most notable, his work for the Kuna people of Panama was complete in 2012, when he and his team accomplished translating the entire Bible for them, allowing them to read and hear God's written Word in their native tongue and heart language.

I was brought to tears when one of his co-laborers, a native of the Kuna people, shared his story of working with Keith in pursuit of following Jesus. With his wife by his side, he spoke of Keith's diligence, passion, and perseverance despite difficulty, lack of resources, and spiritual warfare.

But he spoke of something even more important than Keith's work. He spoke of the work of Almighty God. As he shared about Keith's life and their friendship, I started to grasp the only difference between the Keiths of this world and everyone else: trust. Keith trusted in God more than he trusted in himself. He trusted Him so much that he was willing to put his faith to the test, moving his entire family into the jungles of Panama to do what he heard God tell him to do.

Now while Keith is in heaven celebrating what the Lord was able to do through him, we all get to see the fruit of his trust and daily obedience.

Since 2012, fifteen thousand copies of the Kuna Bible have been printed and distributed, with many more thousands expected in the years to come. The highlight of the funeral for me was learning from his daughter that there are now 40 Kuna missionaries in training to go serve the Lord in Bible translation in South Korea.

To hear that Kuna people, who had never even read God's Word for themselves, would one day be faithfully serving the God who speaks was incredible. Keith's path wasn't easy, and it came with much movement—from South Africa, to Panama, to South Korea. What an unlikely path. But everything accomplished came about because of a faithful God and a man willing to put his faith to the test and trust Him, to take God at His word and daily pursue His call against all difficulties, a lack of resources, and spiritual warfare.

That, my friend, is a story of faithfulness.

But what is faithfulness? To be faithful is to be unwavering and committed regardless of what comes your way. It's having the conviction and steadfastness necessary to accomplish a task and complete a journey.

*In marriage, faithfulness is a willingness to move forward
in purpose toward oneness, regardless of the cost.*

In marriage, faithfulness is a willingness to move forward in purpose toward oneness, regardless of the cost. It's choosing to remain a team, when a trade or a cut, to use sports terms, seems the easier route.

But who should we be faithful to and what is the object of our faith? Well, of course the goal is to be faithful to our spouses. To be committed to them, as our vows say, for richer or for poorer, in sickness and in health. The finish line is at "death do us part."

Our faithfulness needs to be rooted in something bigger, and it must run deeper than our nuptials. Just as it was for Keith Forster, our commitment to faithfulness needs to be directly tethered to God's faithfulness. God alone should be the object of our faith.

Moses, a man who walked with God despite his own personal challenges, sins, and mistakes, spoke well of God's faithfulness when he sang these words in a song to the Israelites shortly before his death:

> He is the Rock, his works are perfect,
> and all his ways are just.
> A faithful God who does no wrong,
> upright and just is he (Deuteronomy 32:4 NIV).

Moses accomplished many things in his life. Most notable, he led the people to the gates of the promised land. But this wouldn't come without much turmoil and worry and many trials and mistakes. Despite setbacks and all-out war, he accomplished the task God laid before him.

Hebrews chapter 11 speaks more about Moses's faith in God, alluding to his decision to be mistreated with the Jewish people instead of benefiting from Egypt's treasure. It speaks much of his courage in the middle of what would be deflating for most of us. This line sums up Moses's faithfulness well: "He regarded disgrace for the sake of Christ as of greater value than the treasures of Egypt, because he was looking ahead to his reward" (Hebrews 11:26 NIV).

Though Moses was born more than a thousand years before Jesus, the Bible describes his willingness to move forward as based in an understanding of and confidence in God's faithfulness in sending Jesus Christ. It says he was sure of the reward he would receive eternally.

Let's take this back to marriage. How many of us are willing to endure like Moses? How many of us are willing to go through war, 40 years in the wilderness, poverty, and despair on our way toward God's will for our marriages and families? Are we willing to trust God this much? Are we willing to believe that looking ahead is worth it?

Our marriages involve us having to deal with only one other human. How would you like to have a whole tribe of people that lacked faithfulness and epitomized the human experience? If God can give Moses the power to be faithful and trust in His faithfulness to lead an entire nation, how much more can He provide that same power to us in our marriages?

Just like Moses couldn't do it on his own, neither can we.

Thankfully, the same Holy Spirit that grants love, joy, peace, patience, kindness, and goodness willingly grants us Christlike faithfulness as well.

For believers, faithfulness is another fruit promised in the presence of God through the Holy Spirit. Though we have a certain amount of faithfulness in our lives by nature because we're made in God's image, the Bible tells us the only way to be filled with this fruit is through His presence.

May the God who granted Moses the power to lead an entire nation of people to the gates of the promised land grant you the power to lead beyond your circumstances and your challenges and into the future and destiny He has for you. May you rely on Him, the One in whom you place your trust as your rock and fortress.

Your Turn

When have you been faithful to a cause where you have remained "all in" despite the difficulty and sheer energy required? How would you compare your faithfulness then to your faithfulness in marriage?

Prayer

Heavenly Father, I've been guilty on many occasions of overestimating my faithfulness in marriage simply because I'm "still here." It's easy to compare myself to someone else and make myself feel better. Thank You for the reminder today that my faithfulness needs to run much deeper than the most basic of definitions. May your Holy Spirit's power give me all I need to embrace the basics of faithfulness and to give my all, regardless of the cost. Remind me that my standard is the very faithfulness of Jesus Christ, who didn't consider equality with You a reason to step back from His mission. May my life reflect a stubborn commitment to my spouse and all You have for us together. In Jesus's name, amen.

17

gentleness

Y ou've read numerous stories in this book about how we have acted toward each other in anger or with a lack of control. You've read about how we've used our instinct, wit, and power against each other. We've laid it all out for you to let you know that we know we are just as much in need of the Holy Spirit's power and fruit as you are.

If we equally need one specific fruit, it's gentleness.

Jonathan

Growing up with a twin brother, I've always been competitive. No matter the activity, I was driven to win. My brother and I would fight often; sometimes for fun and others for keeps. We'd fight with our words, but even more with our fists. He took up boxing in college, and I was a wrestler, so even as late as my early days in marriage, we used the skills we'd acquired in those sports.

I'll never forget the time, just shortly after marriage, when my brother and I decided to get into it, right in front of my new wife.

He had come over to our home, the small and modest second floor of a Victorian house. I don't remember what it was even about, but what started as an argument turned into a scuffle in the middle of our tiny kitchen. I vividly remember my brother pinning me against the kitchen counter, having leapt across the kitchen table to get to me. I should probably mention that my words have always been my first choice of weapon.

The incident was loud and abrasive. The kitchen table scraped across the floor, chairs were knocked over, and glass shattered in the sink as we went from 0 to 100 within a matter of seconds.

We still laugh about it now. Wynter was beside herself, though, not even knowing what to do. It was anything but gentle. She still gets mad at my twin when she thinks about it too long. It's funny, but it does make me feel more loved that she took my side!

Thankfully, I didn't bring this level of intensity into our marriage physically, but I can't say the same for my emotional and audible intensity. Those I brought into marriage, and only the Spirit's power has granted me relief.

Wynter

Jonathan is right. I did take his side, although I was annoyed at both him and his brother for the scene they caused in our new home.

I was beside myself. I grew up with a brother, five years older than me, but I had no idea how to respond to this incident. I told his twin, "Get out of my house!" Both men looked at me as if I were the one who'd lost my mind.

Five minutes later they were fine, though I was still trying to get my emotions in check! It's a twin thing that most of us nontwins don't understand. But I digress.

We both brought a level of intensity into our home that could never be defined as gentleness. Though I desperately wanted Jonathan to be gentle with me, sort of like Richard Gere was with Julia Roberts in *Pretty Woman*, if you know what I mean, gentleness was one trait that eluded us both.

I've already shared how I can be quick with my words and sharp as a knife. But one thing gave us a greater glimpse of God's desired end for us beyond these flaws: our girls.

When God gave us our first daughter, we realized what gentleness is all about—strength under control. Our daughters were all an instant eye-opener for us as we considered our errors and ways in harshness, whether physically, verbally, or emotionally.

Handling and managing our girls has forced us to consider just how gentle someone with power and authority should be.

We'll never forget taking Alena home from the hospital, and it was the same with Kaitlyn, Camryn, and Olivia. With each one of them, as we prepared to leave the hospital, our primary concern was for their well-being and safety. We realized they were delicate and fragile, so we acted accordingly. We had no problem with the hospital's requirement that Wynter leave in a wheelchair, holding the baby. We also welcomed the car seat check the nurse performed to make sure our girls were protected on their first drive. On top of that, on our way home, we managed to drive at our slowest speeds on a major freeway, averaging 20 miles an hour slower than we normally would drive that same road.

When we arrived home, we went out of our way to make sure their tiny little frames were well cared for, having already prepared their bassinets and turned up the heat above where we would normally have it to make sure they weren't cold. That type of care continued, though it lessened at some level as our girls became more independent and self-sufficient.

Even one small cut, bump, bruise, or situation, however, causes us to go right back to extra gentleness in care and a softness that is God breathed naturally to a mommy and daddy.

Oh, how we wish this trait came naturally as we are tasked to care for each other. Our children are already a part of our flesh, and it's most natural to care for them with gentleness and meekness. We gladly check our power and control at the door to make sure they are well cared for.

But as spouses, we're still becoming one. We're learning and trusting God to fill us with this same level of restraint and care that might come more naturally for us with our children.

We both feel vulnerable as we share all this, but we're guessing you might need some help in this area as well.

Just like with all the other fruits, Christ is our example. Check out how the writer of Hebrews describes the length Christ went to, to understand our frailty and weaknesses: "We do not have a high priest who is unable to empathize with our weaknesses, but we have one who has been tempted in every way, just as we are—yet he did not sin" (Hebrews 4:15 NIV).

This should be a shot of confidence for us all! This verse is describing the confidence we should have in our relationship with Christ because He went to the great length of emptying Himself of all His advantages as God to experience the difficulty and weakness of being human. His goal was to experientially understand what it's like to be tempted and to walk with fleshly desires.

Thankfully, as the God-Man, He did not sin, but lived life perfectly, giving Him the ability to be the perfect lamb of God who could be uniquely qualified to pay for the sins of the world.

We cannot imitate Jesus in perfection, but we do have the ability to show empathy. We may not have been tempted in every way, but we have been tempted.

Understanding and empathy lead to gentleness.

The key for us here is that understanding and empathy lead to gentleness.

Jesus knew it well, and He shared, "Take My yoke upon you and learn from Me, for I am gentle and humble in heart, and you will find rest for your souls" (Matthew 11:29 NASB).

How well do you empathize with your spouse, who experiences weaknesses just like you do? How much do you seek to understand the world from their point of view? Are you quick to be rash and to control, or do you take the time to hear them, see them, and humbly seek their best?

None of us are perfect in this regard, but thank God, we can grow!

And thankfully, the same Holy Spirit who grants love, joy, peace, patience, kindness, goodness, and faithfulness willingly grants us Christlike gentleness as well.

For believers, gentleness is another fruit promised in the presence of God through the Holy Spirit. Though we have a certain amount of gentleness in our lives by nature because we are made in God's image, the Bible tells us the only way to be filled with this fruit is through His presence.

May we be a people of prayer who seek to be emptied of all that is harsh and abrasive. May we seek the Holy Spirit's power to be filled with the gentleness of Christ that comes only from understanding empathy.

Your Turn

Think about your interactions with those around you—your coworkers, friends, children, relatives. In what ways have you found it easier to empathize with them? In what ways do you need to empathize with and understand your spouse more? What would it mean to them should you decide to be as gentle as a lamb in your interactions with them?

Prayer

Heavenly Father, thank You for Your great example of gentleness as seen through Christ's willingness to experience pain, hurt, and even death to empathize with me. May I be a spouse—a friend—who is willing to do whatever is necessary to empathize with and understand my spouse. In my understanding, may Your Holy Spirit give me the power to use my words, my emotions, and all that I am to be a soft and warm place for my spouse to find rest. In Jesus's name, amen.

18

Self-Control

We've talked about the different fruits and characteristics of God—the fruits of His Spirit. We've shared how we've fallen short in each of them on many occasions, and how we have had to rely on the Holy Spirit to provide them, daily.

In some ways, perhaps, you might be thinking that, by saying we don't have these characteristics fully supplied naturally, we're offering some type of cop-out, an excuse, for not exuding them in our marriage. You might think we're just trying to make ourselves feel better and we're using our humanity as a crutch. But this couldn't be further from the truth.

Thankfully, the last fruit we'll discuss, another sweet-tasting substance for our marriage and yours, takes away any of those notions: self-control.

It's an interesting word for Paul to use as he discusses life in the Spirit. In some ways, it's a little confusing. Thankfully, God has given us a simple illustration and concept all of us can understand, at least at a basic level.

In the Bible God uses a lot of illustrations with farming words like *planting, sowing, reaping, harvest,* and *seed* throughout. These words are used to describe various aspects of the kingdom, including our own personal growth and development as we follow Jesus.

In 1 Peter 1, Peter is describing holy living and encouraging the believers in Asia Minor who would have been going through great difficulty, including persecution, to live in a way that looks more like Jesus day by day. Remember, holiness is just a simple word that describes what God had in mind when He made us. It's a good word, and to live holy means to live as fully as possible in love, joy, peace, patience, and so on. Need we go on?

But it's likely that his audience would have been discouraged by the standard set in the life of Jesus. Peter spent three years as Jesus's disciple and was a giant in the faith, so how easy would it have been to be intimidated by the words he was sharing. Then Peter makes an interesting statement: "You have been born anew, not of perishable but of imperishable seed, through the living and enduring word of God" (1 Peter 1:23 NRSV).

After all this talk about holy living and sharing about the standard, he comes right back to the only thing powerful enough to help them actually carry out this type of life—God. He says that when they were born again, when they received Jesus, they received an imperishable seed, through the Word of God.

James says it another way in James 1:21: "Get rid of all moral filth and the evil that is so prevalent and humbly accept the word planted in you, which can save you" (NIV).

Both Peter and James refer to the seed being implanted as God's Word, and that it is. But another way to say it is simply like Paul says it in Corinthians: "Do you not know that you are a temple of God and that the Spirit of God dwells in you?" (1 Corinthians 3:16 NASB).

What all three of these authors and disciples of Jesus are saying is that when we receive Jesus, we receive His word. We also receive His Spirit. But we receive it in seed form. As we live in Him and trust Him more, His Spirit grows more and more inside us.

Self-control means growing in Jesus to a point where it becomes difficult to differentiate your spirit from His because you're living in such strong unison.

How would you like to live so that your spouse can't tell you apart from Jesus? Wouldn't it be cool to mistake your spouse for Jesus? This happens only as He, through His Holy Spirit, grows inside us. First John 2:27 says,

> As for you, the anointing that you received from him abides in you, and so you do not need anyone to teach you. But as his anointing teaches you about all things, and is true and is not a lie, and just as it has taught you, abide in him (NRSV).

Once we receive Jesus, we receive His Spirit (His anointing), and as we continue to hang out with Him, we don't need anyone else to teach us! Scripture says His anointing—His Spirit—teaches us about all things! "All things" includes all of Him and all His fruits!

That's what self-control is. It's knowing our teacher, Jesus, to the point of becoming His apprentice.

Jonathan

I can't help but think about *The Karate Kid*. Your mind might go to the more recent film with actor Will Smith's son, Jaden, but mine goes to the old-school 1980s version. The more Daniel gets to know

Mr. Miyagi, the more he observes from his master's life. The more he is trained by him, the more he absorbs his every move. "Wax on! Wax off!" Daniel knows he's not Mr. Miyagi, and Mr. Miyagi knows he's not Daniel. There is a massive difference. But with each fight and with each battle, Daniel stands with more power to win because he has abided in the presence of Mr. Miyagi. He has learned from him. The proverbial seed planted in him, in the form of karate, is growing, and Daniel is experiencing the power of and what it looks like to live with self-control. The skills are not innate to him. They came from Mr. Miyagi, for which Daniel is grateful.

This illustration breaks down at some point, but we hope it helps you understand how we can be in pursuit of self-control. We hope it inspires you as you look to live and act like Jesus in your every move in your marriage.

Jesus's self-control, empowered by the Spirit, allowed Him to stay restrained through the torture, mockery, and even crucifixion He experienced. The Spirit's power enabled Him to choose humility and submission over annihilating His killers.

> Your self-control requires humility and submission.
> Unlike Jesus, you need to know you haven't yet arrived.

Just like for Jesus, your self-control requires humility and submission. Unlike Jesus, you need to know you haven't yet arrived.

You need to be aware that your teacher, the Lord Jesus, has something to teach and impart to you.

But even that humility and submission is a work of God.

Thankfully, the same Holy Spirit, who grants love, joy, peace, patience, kindness, goodness, faithfulness, and gentleness willingly grants us Christlike self-control as well.

For believers, self-control is another fruit promised in the presence of God through the Holy Spirit. Though we have a certain amount of self-control in our lives by nature because we're made in God's image, the Bible tells us the only way to be filled with this fruit is through His presence.

May we be spouses who seek apprenticeship with Jesus Christ by the work of His Spirit. May our marriages exude a willingness to live humbly and submissively before the Lord, so He might empty us of all our false self-sufficiency in exchange for the self-control the Spirit's power provides.

Your Turn

In what ways are you seeking to be mentored by Jesus in self-control? Can someone else in your life teach you the right moves to make in your marriage? Can you take steps toward finding a mentor?

Prayer

Lord Jesus, I desperately want to live a life of self-control, where my spouse can be confident in and reliant on me. I ask You to fill me with the characteristics I need to receive from You. May You give me a humble spirit to receive Your mentorship. May I have eyes that see and ears that hear, and may I receive all You would share toward this end. Bring people into my life who can be Your voice to me, and may I soak in all You've taught them. In Jesus's name, amen.

Part Three

Guided and Directed

19

Looking to Jesus

Most of us have stories about what seemed like random meetings. But take the time to process all the "chance" meetings that had to happen for you to not only meet your spouse, but for you to land where you are today. If you looked hard enough, I bet you would discover that God's hand guided and directed you all along the way.

When we look back at our own story and union, we can't help but think about all the unexpected twists and turns that should not have been. Without them, we wouldn't have met in the first place.

Jonathan

Our paths were supposed to lead to very different places, starting with the fact that I had no intention of attending a university in Philadelphia, but every intention of going to a school in Virginia! I was given a Three-Year Advance Designee Army ROTC Scholarship, which meant I was responsible for the first year of my tuition, but the next three years would be covered if I maintained a certain grade point average. The school in Philadelphia had a rather small ROTC program that was a conglomeration of multiple service branch programs (Army, Navy, Air Force) from across multiple universities throughout the city of Philadelphia. It wasn't the worst program in the country, but it paled in comparison to the Virginia school's prestigious Corp of Cadets.

If the Philly school were my 1989 Toyota Corolla, the Virginia school was a Lexus. It had a rich history of service, selflessness, and tradition that was inspiring to me, having learned the benefits of these characteristics as a Cub Scout and Boy Scout. I had every intention of attending the Virginia school. But the Philly school offered me more money and accepted me earlier. They gave me a deal I couldn't refuse, covering all but a small portion of my first year's tuition. My father made it clear that I would have to make my own way because our financial situation didn't allow him to help me much, so my decision became more about necessity than desire.

Thankfully, I did enjoy the colonel who ran the program in the Philly school. He was a gem of a man and a great leader. Between that and a general intrigue about living in a big city, I reported to the school and their ROTC program directly after Labor Day in 1998. Though we wouldn't meet until three years later, Wynter began as a freshman on the same exact day. We would graduate the same day as well.

On top of that, I entered college knowing that in repayment of my scholarship, I would give Uncle Sam four years of service as an officer in the United States Army. Knowing this, marriage was not clear on my radar. I always thought I would complete my service before contemplating marriage vows. To make matters worse, the events of 9/11 happened just a few weeks prior to Wynter and me meeting, and my seriousness and commitment about my service was never more real and present.

But in the middle of my seriousness and commitment, God dropped this beautiful, intriguing, and confident woman into my life, and she took my attention completely. And in a twist for the ages, less than a year after our meeting, I was discharged from the Army because of a degenerative arthritic condition. I shouldn't have been at Drexel University. I shouldn't have been eligible for marriage. I should have been shipping off for war upon graduation as Operation Iraqi Freedom took most of my friends around the world within months of our graduation in 2003. Instead, two weeks after graduation, Wynter and I said, "I do," and we have the photo on our fireplace mantel to prove it!

Wynter already shared about her post-college plan. It didn't include me, and it didn't include marriage. But God had other plans, and He began to twist, turn, and move our hearts in His direction.

As we think about our story, we can't help but think about everything that needed to line up for us to meet, let alone enter a forever relationship. We mentioned only the highlights, but thousands of details landed us at the exact right time to meet, date, and fall in love.

No story of twists, turns, and moves is greater than the story of Esther in the Bible.

Esther's story is about God's working in history toward unexpected ends He planned years in advance. He had a specific purpose for Esther's life, but the plan was bigger than her. God's name isn't mentioned one time in the book of Esther, but His fingerprints are everywhere in the text. If you've never read it, we beg you to do so sometime soon. It's a short book, only ten chapters in all, but it's power-packed and speaks to the fact that God is always at work, even when we don't see it and expect it the least.

The story revolves around the determination of one man to exterminate the Jews—Haman. Haman's plot might have worked, except for God's weaving seemingly random things together to give Esther favor in the sight of the king. The story recaps her rise from a lowly orphan as a refuge in Babylon, her being raised by her cousin, and then her becoming Queen Esther, seated alongside King Xerxes as one of the most powerful women of her time.

Simply put, Esther was brought to the king's palace because she was a beautiful woman, and Xerxes, despite having many female servants and wives in his harem, chose her as his queen.

The story reeks of randomness, until you get to the end and realize that all the "randomness" was God's plan, done in God's time, for God's purpose. God's interruptions and Esther's obedience partnered to save not only an entire people group, but generations more that would follow after the living God.

But the story doesn't stop there. Through God's salvation of the Jews, yet another time, Jesus Christ would come to be the ultimate Savior for all people who would call on Him as Lord.

Esther wasn't perfect. As far as we know, God's decision to use her wasn't tied to any specific character trait she embodied. Her emotions fluctuated just like anyone's would. She ebbed and flowed between uncertainty and fear for much of the story. But in all her emotions, uncertainty, and fear, Esther trusted God's plan and faithfulness enough to move from uncertainty and fear to confidence and obedience in what she knew He was asking her to do to help save her people.

Have you thought about your life's journey as one that God has been directing behind the scenes, like He did with Esther's? Or do you view it as more random and happenstance? How you answer that question will have far-reaching implications on your journey in marriage. It's the starting point for how you will move forward, and it can not only change your perspective, but history—for good or for bad.

In Esther's story, her cousin Mordecai makes what today is a well-known statement. Esther is questioning her future because her cousin is suggesting she leverage her influence with the king for the benefit of the Jewish people. He wants her to go tell King Xerxes, her husband, that Haman, their adversary, is trying to kill the Jewish people. There is one small problem, though. By going into the king's presence without being summoned, Queen Esther would be defying the law of the land and risking her life. Despite that, her cousin still asks her to go to the king and plead with him on behalf of their people, to vulnerably walk straight into the face of possible calamity. He petitions her to risk her life for the benefit of others. Said another way, he asks her to empty herself of all her royalty, forgetting what she stands to lose, to fulfill God's purpose and preserve something much greater than her life. And then comes the famous line in Esther 4:14. Mordecai says, "If you keep quiet at a time like this, deliverance and relief for the Jews will arise from some other place, but you and your relatives will die. Who knows if perhaps you were made queen for just such a time as this?" (NLT).

A reference in the second sentence is easy to miss. Mordecai starts with "Who knows if perhaps," implying absolute uncertainty and randomness in her position as queen, but then he uses a word we know so well that we miss its implications: *made*. We use it so often and so casually that we forget by using the word, we assume that whatever we are referencing as "made" has to have a "maker." Mordecai is reminding Queen Esther that her position is not random but on purpose. That God had given her a specific purpose, even though he mentions that if she doesn't want to fulfill that purpose, God will find another way. He doesn't leave out the fact that skipping God's purpose will bring about death for her and her relatives. It was her choice, but not following God's plan was not going to end well for her, though following it would also be an uncertain path.

The ending of this story is better than any Hollywood drama you've ever seen. We won't spoil it for you if you've never read it, but we'll give you the obvious: Esther makes a courageous decision to trust God and defy the law of the land to save the Jews. The story has a ton of twists and turns, but she makes a surprising statement of resolve halfway through the book that is a turning point for her story as well as for ours as followers of Jesus Christ. Esther says, "If I must die, I must die" (4:16 NLT).

In this statement, Esther internalizes a reality we must understand if we're going to follow the Lord and His purpose for our lives and our marriages.

She first accepts that her life is not random. Maybe she didn't know it before. We imagine she took her royal status for granted and that she was just happy to be in the palace, eating well and being served. Or maybe she resented her time there. After all, it was a harem, and she wasn't exactly the king's only option for companionship. In either case, in this statement you readily see Esther's understanding that every single thing that had happened in her life had led to this tense moment, and for a reason. She could no longer live a life believing in randomness and coincidence.

But not only does she recognize the deliberateness in her life; she comes to understand that God has a purpose in the deliberateness, that God has a will. It wasn't just a reason; it was a God reason. Esther came to realize that God was orchestrating each step.

After connecting the dots between a reason for being and a God who was making moves, Esther committed her will to God's will even in the face of death. She decided to put it all on the line to accept a call into a story much bigger than her own.

Esther won through accepting a reality that seemed to end in imminent destruction because she trusted the God who can turn imminent destruction into an ending like a fairy tale.

On our marriage journey, we cannot deny God's preordained hand that put us together. The things that had to happen or not happen for us to be together are clearly seen when we look back. We have faced a few moments of perceived destruction that could have ended in death to our joy, death to our intimacy, death to our peace, and even death to our marriage. Yet in these moments, we have learned to say, like Esther, "If I must die, I must die." It hasn't been an easy process, and we're still learning to accept death to fulfill the fairy-tale-like ending planned for us.

We know what you're thinking. *I don't want to die!* Well, neither do we! Thankfully, we aren't necessarily talking about physical death, but figurative death (though God does call some to die for a spouse, but rarely). Yet He is calling us to die to anything and everything that is not of His Spirit and to whatever keeps His Spirit from growing inside of us.

We know this is difficult, and we have shared our own failures in this dying. But we have found that dying to what seems most natural so we can gain the supernatural means we will continue the journey toward a story even more thrilling than we've imagined.

The story of Esther gives us a great example of someone willing to give their life for someone else. For Esther, it was so thousands of others could live. Where did she muster that kind of strength? That's the question we must ask.

Most of us put Esther on a pedestal, as if she were superhuman, but it's clear that Esther was just a regular person like us. Yes, she had specific qualities that made her right for the time—mainly her beauty. Her attractiveness gave her proximity to the king, but other than that, nothing set her apart or made her a superhero.

So where did her strength come from? The answer to that questions is found at the very top of her story arc:

> Then Esther sent this reply to Mordecai: "Go and gather together all the Jews of Susa and fast for me. Do not eat or drink for three days, night or day. My maids and I will do the same. And then, though it is against the law, I will go in to see the king" (4:15-16 NLT).

Though this story never mentions God, these few sentences are telling about where Esther looked for her strength. We have to imagine that she felt smaller than an ant as she looked at the task ahead of her, and we can't help but believe that she was afraid and insecure. In fact, based on Mordecai's conversation with her, we can infer that her greatest concern was for her own life. And we get it! If the shoes were on our feet, we would likely feel the same!

All that said, Esther tells Mordecai and all the Jews in the land to fast. The only reason she would ask them not to eat is so they could use the time to hunger for God's help and presence. That's the main purpose for fasting in Jewish culture, and it's true for us as Christians today.

Fasting. Prayer. Dependence on God.

Esther doesn't make her well-known statement, "If I must die, I must die," until she first throws her very life at the feet of God. She knows that only through God's will will she be able to carry out what she commits to—if necessary, to her death.

She is asking God to intercede for her and her people.

If you have any faith in God, you can't help but get fired up by this thought! Who wouldn't want this type of faith? Who wouldn't want the strength and courage to take a road that could lead to death to bring about a fairy-tale-like ending? Of course we want this! The only problem is finding the courage.

Just like Esther, we will find that courage only in a life completely dependent on God.

Fasting. Prayer. Dependence on God.

Just like Esther, our fairy-tale-like ending is waiting for us to throw ourselves at the feet of God. Our arc hits its climax when we make a conscious decision to submit our greatest fears, worries, problems, and the evil stored up in our hearts (Luke 6:45), and to throw those things at the very feet of a God who is willing to step in.

God proved Himself over and over to the Israelites in the Old Testament. His promised presence to them was like a buoy on the stormy ocean of life. The Jewish people held on to numerous Scriptures. One of our favorites we also cling to is in Deuteronomy, when the Lord says through Moses, "Be strong and courageous! Do not be afraid and do not panic before them. For the LORD your God will personally go ahead of you. He will neither fail you nor abandon you" (Deuteronomy 31:6 NLT).

Regardless of the storms they would face, and regardless of the evil that would come against them, the people knew they could rely on the very real and present God in their darkest days. He was there for them personally.

As Christians, we have this same promise, but God made His presence all the more real to the world in the person of Jesus Christ.

In the final chapter of the book of Hebrews in the New Testament, as he speaks about moral obligations in marriage, the author also draws a final encouragement from an Old Testament promise from God in Psalm 118:6:

> Let marriage be held in honor among all, and let the marriage bed be undefiled, for God will judge the sexually immoral and adulterous. Keep your life free from love of money, and be content with what you have, for he has said, "I will never leave you nor forsake you." So we can confidently say,
>
> "The Lord is my helper;
> I will not fear;
> what can man do to me?" (Hebrews 13:4-6).

The author starts by speaking very plainly about what our marriages should look like:

Honor. We wish we could say honor comes naturally, but how often do we get this wrong, and how easy is it to dishonor our spouses? In conversations with each other or in how we talk about our spouse to a friend, this isn't always the easiest directive to follow.

Pure. Even if you can claim purity of actions regarding your spouse, how often has your mind drifted into impure thoughts about someone else?

Okay, so say you're batting two for two and you have kept your relationship honorable at all times and pure in the sight of

God? Have you failed at pursuing happiness in marriage? I think I stumped you here, because I'm 100 percent sure you haven't been perfectly happy in your marriage. Play the reel backward, even if just intermittently.

The standard is extremely high, and the bar is out of reach. If you've followed Jesus for more than a few years, I'm sure you've figured that out.

That is why Esther is such a strong example for us! She executed the plan God had for her, with amazing results. Her story ends happily! Fortunately for Esther, the Scripture records her success. We can infer from Scripture that she might have had some failures along the way, but we're positive that if we get to talk to her in heaven, we'll learn God's hand filled in the gaps she left in her quest for perfection.

That's why we love what the author of Hebrews shares after giving us a few guidelines for marriage. Before he quotes our verse from Deuteronomy we're sure Esther leaned on, he draws from Deuteronomy 31:6 when he says, "He has said, 'I will never leave you nor forsake you'" (Hebrews 13:5).

These verses remind us as New Testament believers that we can put the same level of dependence on God Esther did when she trusted Him with her life. The Lord helps us to be bold and courageous. God Himself causes us not to be afraid.

The author of Hebrews even refers back to other leaders, like Esther, whose stories give us a level of faith in God to take Him at His word:

> Remember your leaders, those who spoke to you the word of God. Consider the outcome of their way of life, and imitate their faith. Jesus Christ is the same yesterday and today and forever (Hebrews 13:7-8).

Think about how Esther put it all on the line, even in the face of death, to accomplish the plan God had for her and His people. Internalize that thought, and then copy her faith. Choose to put it all on the line. Choose to face death to your plans, death to your fears, death to whatever evil is stored up in your heart, death to anything that could cause you to falter.

Choose to be emptied. Choose to be poured out.

Choose to be emptied. Choose to be poured out. Choose to die to all these things, knowing you can put your full dependence on the One who will give your marriage the twists and turns necessary to have that happy ending after you let go.

The author is explicit about who this God is when he shares, "Jesus Christ is the same yesterday and today and forever" (Hebrews 13:8).

He is dependable. He is trustworthy. Though Esther is a great example, Jesus is the greatest example for what putting it all on the line looks like.

Most often our marriages aren't filled with decisions that seem as important as Esther's was. Her decision held life and death in the balance for a whole nation of people. But what if we considered what's at stake when we enter marriage? No doubt, our decisions can be just as weighty as hers. The greatest difference between Esther's decision and yours is that you don't get to read your story until after it's written. Her story is already written. Yours is still being made.

Esther is also a great example for us as we consider the purpose God has for us in life and marriage. She threw her life on the line, trusting in a God who was writing her story. As we've said, she wasn't perfect. She wasn't better or more important than we are. Her life was just as complicated and messy. But two ideas that exemplify her life would change our lives if we internalized and operated from them.

Dependence

Obedience.

Marriage wasn't the focus of Esther's story, but the illustrations we can draw from her story should absolutely make an impact on the way we think about and operate in our marriages.

As much as we pursue dependence on God and obedience to His call and plan, we're focused on those same two specific keys to Esther's victory. She was dependent on the Lord to provide her protection, favor, success—and life itself when death seemed inevitable.

Esther's story is a great reminder to all of us as we continue the journey of marriage.

Her story is an encouragement on so many levels, starting with the fact that her story is God's story. God's sovereign hand runs continuously throughout her story, reminding each of us that He is always working, even when we least expect it. He is working in the good, and He is working in the bad. He is working in the small things, and He is working in the seemingly grand things. God is interested and involved in every aspect of life. Romans 8:28 reminds us, "We know that for those who love God all things work together for good, for those who are called according to his purpose."

Yes, His goodness motivates Him, and we can rely on this very fact. His heart is for us, and we can trust Him to be faithful, even as we ask Him to help us to be faithful. He will interrupt, and He will inconvenience. He will call, and He will command. But even in His call, He is thinking about our good.

His interest is in our joy, though He knows it will often come only with patience and endurance. Most often, the things He asks us to do seem to come only with our willingness to submit and to die to what we want and think we deserve and can't live without.

But even in the tests and trials, we can find His peace. We can be confident that His perfect peace will guard our hearts, and that though the storms rage all around us, our minds and hearts can be secure.

We can trust that He will lead us with gentleness, and that even when we slip and fall His kindness will be our support. In all that we're going through, He is teaching us self-control.

Esther's story is a reminder to us that God has a grand purpose and a plan. We've been married long enough to see God's hand at work. We can look back at all we've been through and see God weaving it all together. He has used our good, our bad, and our ugly along the way, and He has challenged us to die to the things that once held us hostage and sought to destroy our marriage. His Holy Spirit has been calling us to live more and more like Jesus every day. Thankfully, He is giving us the power we need to emulate Him.

We are more committed than ever to asking God to fill us with His power, to empty ourselves and pour ourselves out for each other, so He can fill us up with more of Him and His fruit.

We are more committed than ever to asking God to fill us with His power to empty ourselves and pour ourselves out for each other, so He can fill us up with more of Him and His fruit. We are looking to Jesus, the author and perfecter of our faith, knowing that He alone will move us continually toward His will.

Our prayer is that you will do the same. We pray you will look to

Jesus, trusting earnestly for His Spirit to fill you with His power so you can pour yourselves out until you are empty, so He can fill you with the fullness of His Spirit—His love, joy, peace, patience, kindness, goodness, faithfulness, gentleness, and self-control.

I thank my God every time I remember you. In all my prayers for all of you, I always pray with joy because of your partnership in the gospel from the first day until now, being confident of this, that he who began a good work in you will carry it on to completion until the day of Christ Jesus.

PHILIPPIANS 1:3-6 NIV

About the Authors

Wynter Pitts is the author of several books, including *You're God's Girl!* She is the founder of *For Girls Like You*, a bimonthly magazine that equips girls to walk boldly into who God has created them to be and to resource their parents to raise strong Christ-following God girls that say yes to His plans for their lives. Wynter tragically passed from death to life on July 24, 2018, after 15 years of marriage to her beloved Jonathan. She leaves behind an incredible legacy through her many writings but more importantly in her four daughters—Alena, Kaitlyn, Camryn, and Olivia.

Jonathan Pitts is an author, speaker, and executive pastor at Church of the City in Franklin, TN. Prior to pastoring, Jonathan was executive director at The Urban Alternative, the national ministry of Dr. Tony Evans in Dallas, Texas. Jonathan lives in Franklin, Tennessee with his four daughters.